CLIP TOENAILS FOR A LIVING

DR. MARCIN N. VACLAW

CLIP TOENAILS FOR A LIVING

A UNIQUE PATH TO

COPYRIGHT © 2025 MARCIN N. VACLAW
All rights reserved.

CLIP TOENAILS FOR A LIVING
A Unique Path to Success

FIRST EDITION

ISBN 978-1-5445-4913-2 *Hardcover*
      978-1-5445-4912-5 *Paperback*
      978-1-5445-4911-8 *Ebook*
      978-1-5445-4910-1 *Audiobook*

To my family, who made me who I am.

To my wife, who loves me in spite of who I am.

And to Casey, who inspired and pushed me to write this.

CONTENTS

INTRODUCTION 9

PART 1: THE FOUNDATION OF SUCCESS
1. THE BREAD AND BUTTER 23
2. EMBRACING THE GRIND 43
3. THE PIVOT 67

PART 2: BUILDING YOUR UNIQUE PATH TO SUCCESS
4. THE REWARD OF EFFORT 101
5. THE IMPORTANCE OF DIFFERENTIATION 117
6. LEVERAGING THE STRENGTHS OF OTHERS 135
7. THE USEFULNESS OF DISCOMFORT 149
8. FAIL IN ORDER TO SUCCEED 165

PART 3: THE PROCESS OF SUCCESS
9. DEFINE YOUR OWN SUCCESS 185
10. ALWAYS TAKING ACTION 197

ACKNOWLEDGMENTS 209
ABOUT THE AUTHOR 211

INTRODUCTION

A RECIPE FOR SUCCESS

"You can have a recipe for success, but you still have to cook."
—UNKNOWN

Sibling rivalries can be a wonderful thing.

I'm the seventh of eight highly competitive siblings. We aren't the type of siblings who talk every day on the phone. But when we're together, it's so much fun. We get to catch up and re-create the loud, energetic environment like when we were kids.

I love spending time with them.

During these visits we often gather around a kitchen table enjoying delicious food. Often, I enjoy pitting my siblings against each other to make *me* good food.

For instance, some of my siblings think they make the "world's best" chocolate chip cookie dough. So as we talk and catch up, at some point early on, I'll goad them a little bit. All I have to say is, "Amy, have you ever had Russell's cookie dough? It's so good!"

If I'm not stopped mid-sentence, it'll only take a few moments before my siblings are pulling ingredients out of the pantry, withholding *the* secret of their own recipes, razzing each other about why *this* or *that* detail of another's recipe is wrong, and gloating about why their recipe is the best.

Because they're feeling competitive, they spill *some* details. One sibling swears by mixing in crumbled Biscoff cookies. Another likes to add just a hint of cinnamon. Just a small amount. Nothing that'll overpower the taste. A third adds a touch of cream cheese to make it more rich. My brother Russ sets himself apart by adding Ghirardelli's sea salt and caramel chocolate squares. And one sibling is the traditionalist who sticks with the tried-and-true recipe, keeping it simple—there's always one.

Some still refuse to give up their secrets. In doing recipe research for this book, one sibling responded to my call by saying, "You don't just ask for my cookie dough recipe. You have to earn the right to enjoy them. If you want me to make you cookies, you just have to ask. But it's okay. I'll do it next time you're here."

Each feels competitive. Each is staunch in their beliefs. None of them is wrong.

GOOD THINGS COME TO THOSE WHO MAKE

Meanwhile, after I've set the wheels in motion, I sit back as the soon-to-be beneficiary of this cookie-dough rivalry.

Why just the dough and not cookies? Cookie dough is all you'd ever get in a house with eight kids. My mom would *try* to bake us cookies. But with eight mouths, the dough usually never made it to the oven—sneaky hands would shoot up and snag a ball of dough off the counter. Even though we're adults now, that habit hasn't changed. I mean, it's cookie dough. It's delicious.

Once my siblings' dough is complete, I get to sample their work. Sure, there are opinions. But each ball of dough served is mouthwatering. And I get to enjoy them with my family. In other words, another *successful* family visit.

Over time, successfully getting cookie dough has helped me reflect on success and what gets us there. In the end, there is no one specific way to make delicious cookie dough. Or to char a steak. Or to mix mashed potatoes. Or to open a successful business. There is never one single recipe that gets it right. It will be different for everybody.

Each of us might use relatively similar ingredients, but everyone can put their own culinary flair into how a recipe is prepared. Success isn't a singular recipe of "add this measured amount" or "mix in *this* after *that*." There are, in fact, countless ways to find success—and they are each valid paths. Ingredients that worked for me will be the focus of this book.

COOKING FROM OUR OWN RECIPES

That there are multiple paths to success is true beyond making cookie dough.

Just take my siblings. One sibling has found success not just with his cookie dough but as an attorney and now a district judge. Two other brothers are successful businessmen in the oil and gas industry. My two sisters are successful in the travel and aesthetics industries. My oldest brother has a family practice clinic. We are each different, and our success is different. On their unique journeys, they've combined different ingredients to find their success, redefining it to fit their own values and outlooks. When you add it all up, everything in their life is a recipe that has led to them, individuals I'm proud to call my siblings.

Your proverbial cookie dough recipe is just as valid. Maybe it has chocolate squares. Maybe it doesn't. Success can be what you want it to be. *You* get to set your own standards.

So what does your recipe look like? That's what I hope to help you figure out. And I'm here to tell you that finding your unique recipe to success is within reach. But don't get too excited yet. From my experience, that process can be a challenge. If it were as easy as some formula, then everyone could be successful without much effort.

But there are things that have worked for me that I'd like to share with you. For example, I find success emanates from where we can differentiate ourselves from the crowd—when we realize what can make us unique.

When you determine what makes you unique, that's when it's time to cook. Create the circumstances where you explore and find what works for you. Goad yourself into self-improvement the same way I goad my siblings to find the perfect cookie dough.

Rinse and repeat. Then bon appétit.

A SECRET INGREDIENT

It's important to shift our mindset and realize that there is an infinite number of pathways to success. Why? Quite simply, there are misconceptions surrounding the traditional narratives of success.

For example, one traditional pathway to success has been through formal schooling. The idea follows that the more years you accumulate in "higher" education, the more successful you can expect to be. But many people—small business owners, folks in the middle of their career, and even doctors—are finding themselves working hard and not on track with the success they wanted or hoped to have. Whether you go to medical school or trade school, that narrow path does not necessarily equate to financial reward.

Nor does it automatically create other forms of success, such as family success, physical and mental success, work-life balance success, or however you might define your ideal life. So there have to be more ingredients in "the recipe for success" that we were never given.

When that surprise hits, we can feel stuck. We start asking ourselves tough questions. *Did I make the best choice for my career? How am I going to retire? What will my future look like? How am I going to get through the rest of this?* Before long, we can feel burdened by the hamster wheel of daily life. And it's a recipe that gets stale after a while.

It can be a little bit like *Groundhog Day*—that feeling of living the same day over and over again. Here's what my hamster wheel might look like as a doctor: For each patient interaction, I sit down in front of somebody, listen to the nuance of their medical complaints, objectively sort through those details, come up with a diagnosis and describe it to them for their own education, and then help them fix the problem or, at the very least, make it better. I repeat this process for every one of the dozens of patients I see in a day. Then I wake up the next day and do it all over again. Until I retire.

This can be true of any occupation. Take mechanics. A client walks into their place of business and states a complaint about a car. The car is diagnosed. The mechanic explains the diagnosis, and the issue can hopefully be fixed. Builders, executives, managers, teachers, engineers, and stay-at-home parents all go through a similar monotony. Until they retire.

Day in and day out, repetition can get monotonous.

For the self-employed and career-focused, this cycle makes for long days at work and, sometimes, a difficulty to see our own success. It spreads us thin, chips away at our self-confidence and self-worth, and generally overwhelms us with responsibility. It can prevent us from reaching our potential. And with enough pressure and time, any passion we had for work wanes. It starts to feel like a means to an end.

When this happens, you may think that you're stuck in a rut. That you're not growing and you're missing out on success. In reality, you are actually in the process of being successful. You're still making your cookie dough.

So where does a spark of change, growth, and gratitude come from? Here's one way: We can start to recognize the value of the grinding work we do day in and day out. This realization is just one secret ingredient that is seldom taught.

How can the grind help us? Let's look at the rainbow through the storm. What does hard work get us? Notice that there's a rewarding arc to the grind I just described. Doctors like myself are literally helping people—taking away their pain or targeting a specific outcome. That's a rewarding outcome, and a positive one.

That same positive outcome exists within every other occupation, too. The daily lesson planning of teachers helps their students' minds grow. The torquing, oil-staining labor of mechanics helps their clients' cars and lives run smoothly. The never-ending physical and technical training of astronauts helps them further humanity's understanding of the universe. We could go on. There is almost always a magnificent outcome for what is otherwise a painful grind. That realization can inspire us to do more.

So update your recipe for success by adding an ingredient: the value of the grind.

ADJUST YOUR RECIPE

When adjusting your own recipe, I've found that being okay with wherever you are now, understanding and seeking out new growth opportunities, and discovering the pathway that will help you achieve your goals.

Keep in mind that your plans and goals will (or should) be unique to you. And they should be inspirational—something achievable that motivates you to cultivate who you are. And they'll be adjusted over time.

A pilot once told me that, at takeoff, if the plane is off by one degree from its destination and is never course-corrected, that plane will end up hundreds of miles away from its intended target. That opened my eyes to the constant adjustments and careful planning that are essential ingredients for following a unique path and landing somewhere successfully.

What is your definition of success? Only you can answer that question. It could be a simple motivation to read your next book. It could be a radical change to your business plan. Or anything in between. Regardless, it will lead to actionable steps that lead to personal growth.

To help you in your journey, and in Part 1, we'll explore the fundamentals and how big successes are actually a series of little successes. Included in that is doing the unglamorous, bread-and-butter work that leads to the life you envision and desire. But, of course, things don't always go as planned, which is why this section of the book will conclude with "the pivot," or the skill of adjusting to new circumstances on the fly.

In Part 2, we'll build on those ingredients. First, we'll learn about the grind and utilizing it to get to where you want to be. From there, we'll turn to the importance of differentiating yourself. There is power in finding your niche. Afterward, we'll face the truth that, as much as you are important to your own success, you'll need to surround yourself with amazing people. It's a sure-fire way to accelerate your own journey. There are always obstacles, discomfort, and failures to overcome on any journey. You'll learn how these don't hold us back, they actually launch us forward.

Whether you're a podiatrist or a plumber, Part 3 will reveal that success isn't about *what* you do, it's about doing it well. Here, we'll circle back to the fact that there's no single recipe or definition for success, and how to overcome the stifling narratives of traditional success that bring us down. And to close it out, we'll discover that, even when major goals are met, there are always new horizons to explore. The book's end will be another beginning—thinking about the next chapter.

By the time you've turned the last page, you'll have the ingredients I've used to become successful. For me, they've added value without diminishing growth, innovation, or improvement. Along the way, I hope you are imbued with a sense that "I can do this!" Where there was uncertainty and monotony, there will instead be a feeling that it's possible to be the best at anything you encounter during your unique journey.

LET ME BE YOUR SOUS-CHEF

And there's a reason why I'm stressing *unique*. Your uniqueness will be the strength to your own self-improvement. Do you know how I know that? I'm living that truth.

Despite my own successes, I am not any more exceptional than anybody else. My own journey is unique, just like yours. I had to adjust, find a niche, and master the fundamentals.

My original plan was to go back to my hometown and take over my father's dental practice. After a long list of variables, obstacles, encounters, and experiences, I came to the hard realization that dentistry was not meant for me after all.

A friend of mine suggested podiatry. At first I was unsure, so I called a few podiatry schools. In short order, I got a dean of admissions on the phone who asked me to fly out and tour the school. My pivot revealed a much more inviting path.

After finishing four years of podiatric medical school in Ohio, I did my residency in Texas. In my last year, circumstances gave me time and energy to focus on the future. So I set a goal to start a practice as soon as I graduated from residency.

Two days after graduating, I saw eight patients.

Of course, there were obstacles before that happened. But I embraced the value of hard work. First, I had to develop a business plan. And there are no Business Plan 101 classes in med school. That meant I had to teach myself.

And in order to wait months to get on insurance plans—to get paid for my work—I had to go through a complex process. To get the ball rolling on that process, I needed my residency diploma. Well, the stinger was that residency diplomas aren't made available immediately after graduation. Typically they're issued around June 30 even if the program ended months prior.

So with goals and obstacles in front of me, what did I do? I thought outside the box and devised a plan.

About a month before I graduated, there was this residency graduation dinner for all the residents, directors, and attendings in Houston. We still had weeks left in our residency, but the dinner signaled our soon-to-be-achievement of graduation. A fun send-off at a fancy restaurant. A planned part of the festivities was to take an official picture with our residency director while holding, wait for it, a signed copy of our diploma.

I told my wife about this. And instead of waiting for my

copy, I asked her to sneak a photo of me holding the diploma. She did! I made a copy of the photo and put it in my application for the insurance payers. It gave me a four-week head start. Around a month later, and two days after graduation, I was approved. Thinking outside the box, I pivoted by coming up with a creative solution that helped me get over a significant obstacle to my dream.

I owned a growing podiatry clinic. Success.

Now I'm several stops—and several successes—later on the path. Currently, I serve as the chief medical officer of Allevio, a comprehensive healthcare support service designed to optimize the operations of podiatry clinics and other healthcare practices, and executive chairman of Allevio's Medical Advisory Board. To date, it's one of the largest podiatry groups in the United States. Although my journey might sound glamorous, it actually required working hard and the decidedly unglamorous concept of clipping toenails for a living.

Every step on this journey has been part of a unique recipe for success, one that has essential parts I'd like to share with you. With these ingredients I present here, they'll then be yours to enhance and tailor to your own liking.

WHAT DOES "CLIP TOENAILS FOR A LIVING" MEAN?

But before we get going, I want to talk to you about the philosophy behind "Clip Toenails for a Living," one of the mantras that has influenced my continued growth. What does it mean?

We'll explore it in more detail. But it means a willingness to do what many think is unglamorous. It means that success requires that you follow your unique path by finding your niche and differentiating yourself. It means you need to do the fundamental things well.

Let's be honest. Toenails are gross. Yet toenails are a fundamental part of podiatry. It's not flashy. It's not an innovative new surgery technique or a groundbreaking new piece of medical equipment. Nor is it extremely profitable.

But clipping toenails became a major part of what makes my story different from other podiatrists. It's in my unique recipe. I found a niche way to marry clipping toenails, foot examinations, and house calls. My life—and everything I've accomplished professionally—is built from clipping fungal, brittle, bacterial, ridged, splitting, and ingrown toenails.

To find success, you'll need to clip toenails, too. In other words, you'll need to wade through the unglamorous to recognize your secret ingredients. And you get to experiment with a recipe that works for you.

But don't get me wrong. This book is not a blueprint for success. It's not an algorithm or equation. Instead, it's a series of anecdotes from one podiatrist in Texas. It's a revelation that, within you, there is a pathway to success that will not apply to anyone else.

So what are you waiting for? Use this book as a tool for growth. Use it for motivation. Use it for inspiration. Use it to evolve your recipe for success.

I'm grateful you're here, and it's my pleasure to share my secret ingredients with you. And it starts with seeing the value in small things. Let's get cooking!

PART 1

THE FOUNDATION OF SUCCESS

CHAPTER 1

THE BREAD AND BUTTER

"Do the common thing uncommonly well."

—JOHN D. ROCKEFELLER

My mom put a lot of work every night into feeding her eight kids. Sometimes the neighborhood kids, too.

Growing up, my favorite meal that she made was chicken fried steak. But whatever she made, it would always be accompanied by a variety of delicious sides. I can picture the whole table now. There'd be baked potatoes or mashed potatoes. Also a roasted veggie like carrots, broccoli, or handpicked green beans from my Aunt Annie's farm. And, of course, some type of salad that nobody touched.

No matter what the sides were, there'd also be bread and butter. Maybe the bread was homemade crescent rolls, garlic bread, rosemary rolls, a sliced baguette, or some type of savory pull-apart. Regardless, there'd always be bread and butter with every meal. That's just the way it was.

Bread and butter accompanied everything, and without them, the meal wouldn't be complete.

But bread and butter are rarely the star of the show, even if it's on a sandwich. Nobody has ever said, "Have you ever had Mom's peanut butter and jelly sandwich? The bread is to die for." No. The main ingredients are favored. They're called *main* ingredients for a reason. Yet, despite being out of the limelight, bread and butter are foundational components—the unsung heroes, one could say—of our diet.

They are the smaller components that *make* the meal work. They are the underappreciated things that do the heavy lifting. And that's why, as part of our shared colloquialisms, "the bread and butter" is a saying used to signify the underlying and most important part of a larger thing. What's true of my childhood dinner table is also true of our success in life: If mastered, the "bread and butter" can provide the main, foundational part of any reward.

Big things are built on the little things. Solid foundations can help us develop a process of success. Gears become bikes. Bikes become cars. Cars become rockets.

FOUNDATIONAL FOOTING

Foundational things are crucial. A foundation is something you can stand on. As a podiatrist, I can tell you that having healthy feet turns out to be a very foundational part of a functioning human body.

Leonardo da Vinci famously said, "The human foot is a masterpiece of engineering and a work of art." They are the appendages that make contact with the ground, the first line of defense to protect us from the dust and danger of the world. They're the belly of a boat, riddled with must, rust, and slime.

Calloused and soiled, the bare foot assumes the entire burden of your body's load, from your first step to your last.

Dressed in the adornments of our finest materials—shoes, socks, and sometimes rings—the feet are an ox in an evening gown.

But almost every other body part *seems* much more important to us. You have a brain, a heart, and intricate systems, like the cardiovascular system, within your body that are the main ingredients—the things that get the most attention. Our eyes see the world. Our ears hear the world. Our mouths speak, giving us the power to express ourselves. Feet aren't thought of in these grandiose terms. Consider it yourself. When you think about your health, do you think of your feet as more important than your heart? Of course not.

Feet are even second fiddle to our hands. Although they are both similar, the hands are so much more dextrous. Our hands are our catchall tools. Hands play the guitar, type on the keyboard, or begin a relationship or an encounter with a handshake. Compared to hands, feet almost seem irrelevant.

This irrelevance aligns with our own anatomy. The feet are the farthest thing from your heart, getting the very last of the nourishment that comes through the circulatory system. They get the leftovers. And because of gravity, they struggle to push things back up to the rest of our body.

Yet, in order to stand, we need our feet. When not attended to, elite feet will be aching, sore, and immobile. As a podiatrist, I've seen people come up against a brick wall, health-wise, when they have foot problems. What that tells us is this: Even the most neglected and unglamorous parts of our lives merit attention and care. Moreover, if those smaller details are not accounted for and taken care of, you won't be able to walk, let alone run.

Feet are the tires on a car. A Ferrari is a Ferrari, but if it has a flat tire, it doesn't matter how awesome the engine is. That car is going nowhere. When we injure our feet—the underappreciated bread and butter that keeps our body going—that's a whole new ball game. If we have to put our foot in a boot or resign ourselves to a wheelchair, walking becomes difficult or impossible. That's when things change in our mind. We start realizing that we can't even take a single step forward, something we need to do thousands of times each day to live our lives.

THE UNSUNG HEROES

The feet are our unsung heroes. And within podiatry itself, there are further underappreciated, foundational treatments. So, when I was a podiatrist in training, I took a long, hard look at the foundational, bread-and-butter elements of my work—the common, unsung components that, if I mastered them, could lead to the most substantial reward.

That underappreciated work, I discovered, was a combination of foot examinations and clipping toenails—what we call *toenail management*. The vast majority of podiatry is managing toenail problems. If that was the underappreciated work, what was the sought-after work? Surgeries, lecture circuits, or inventing new techniques or devices are the sexy parts of the job. The things everybody clamors for. The things that people aspire to.

But the bread-and-butter need for patients is clipping toenails. With age, nails change much like our hair and skin. Dexterity worsens. Reaching the feet gets more difficult. Toenails get thicker, harder, and are more susceptible to becoming fungal or infected as our immune system weakens. Because very few people think of their feet as important—instead, getting colonoscopies, hip replacements, and heart checkups, which are also important—many patients let their toenails get out of control. At that point, they'll need the professional intervention of a podiatrist every few months.

Part of me wants to insert a few pictures into this book to show you how nasty toenails can get. But I get the feeling that just mentioning it lets your imagination do that work. These toenail issues debilitate patients to the point that they cannot function in their day-to-day lives—just because their toenails get out of control.

So, like the tires on a Ferrari, clipping toenails ends up being the foundation, bread and butter of podiatry. Not surgeries, not device invention, nor going on the lecture circuit. That was revelatory to me. Finding success, for me, meant starting from a strong foundation and learning to do the necessary, unglamorous things well.

I'm clipping toenails, managing problematic nails, and keeping my patients walking.

Simple things are not difficult, but they are often ignored or forgotten. As I've said, people tend to forget to take care of their feet. And likewise, podiatrists don't often see the value of clipping toenails. When I started doing the bread-and-butter work well and nailed the fundamentals (pun intended), that's when my practice took off.

MASTERING THE FUNDAMENTALS

When you look at the most successful people in the world, they tend to master the fundamentals.

That's what the greatest basketball player in the history of the game, Michael Jordan, did. He could do things no other player could, such as drain an off-balanced, game-winning jump shot over Bryon Russell while falling backward. True story. But he could do those kinds of amazing things because he mastered the fundamentals.

In the first part of Michael Jordan's book *Rare Air*, he talks about his practice routine in excruciating detail. He also reveals how his routine surprised people. The surprise came from the fact that he would not practice by simulating a game-winning shot scenario or the extraordinary things we now associate with the greatest basketball player of all time. Instead, the bulk of his practice routine consisted of dribbling, shooting layups, and shooting free throws—things that are considered the "easiest" part of playing basketball. He was focused on mastering the unglamorous, forgotten fundamentals. The small and simple things. He knew that if he was the best at those, he could beat anybody. He could dribble past them and know he'd never miss a shot whether it was at the start of the game or the game-winning buzzer beater.

I don't know if Patrick Ewing, Karl Malone, John Stockton, Hakeem Olajuwon, Reggie Miller, or Gary Payton were practicing their layups. And we know, just looking at the numbers, that Shaquille O'Neal never practiced free throws. (Love you, Shaq.) And that is partly why they couldn't beat Mike.

Ray Lewis has a similar approach. The Hall of Fame NFL linebacker had to be strong to excel in his position. It turns out that his iconic jersey number—52—is linked to his mastering-fundamentals approach. As a child, Lewis was deeply affected by witnessing his mother suffer abuse at the hands of his stepfather. Some day, Lewis knew he might be strong enough to defend her. To do that, he'd take a deck of cards—all fifty-two of them—and flip through them. Whatever numbers came up, he'd perform as many push-ups and sit-ups as were on the card values. He did ten push-ups for face cards, twenty-five for aces, and fifty for jokers. No matter how difficult, he was determined to build a foundation of toughness through a fundamental training process.

Turning over the cards again and again, he'd get through all fifty-two cards and then start again. That was his workout. Then, that number emblazoned his jersey as a representation of his determination.

Ignoring the fundamentals won't push you into that upper echelon, won't get you the success that you could otherwise achieve. So master those fundamentals. End of story.

In my field, the under-appreciation of managing toenails has made podiatry necessary and important all across the country. It's not glamorous. Certainly not as glamorous as the operating room where ankle scopes, tendon repairs, and tendon transfers are a wondrous mixture of teamwork, skill, and science. It's not as glamorous as the lecture circuit, which gives a doctor some well-earned bragging rights. Nobody brags about clipping toenails. It's often looked down upon, in a way, making it as ignored in podiatry as much as toenails get ignored by patients.

Clipping toenails is my version of dribbling and layups and push-ups. It's a small and simple thing that doesn't take the most skill or talent. But when I chose to excel at those foundational things, it became the bread and butter of my practice and the most valuable part of my unique skillset. (I often say that everyone on earth has something that they could contribute in an apocalyptic event. Some can hunt food. Some can build and repair or tinker with electronics. Others can garden and cook. My contribution would be my ability to clip toenails.)

The same is likely true for your field, too. A chef at a pizza shop can have the best toppings in the world, but the dough is the foundation of a good pizza. If they don't master the fundamentals of the dough, the rest of the pizza won't matter. Nobody will want to eat it. Or, geologists can expound forever on natural disasters and the massive scale of tectonic plates, but they can also pick up an ordinary rock out of a garden and use it to tell you the extensive history of the local area. It's just a rock, yet they can do so much with it. What's a seemingly unimportant thing to most is the foundation of their knowledge.

What are your field's foundational skills? The bread and butter can be the most valuable part of your skillset. In other words, never overlook the value of the small, foundational things.

From the small things, you can build much bigger things.

BUILDING ON THE SMALL THINGS

Many people know me as the "House Call Foot Doctor." Before that happened, I met Dr. Larry Anthon. I credit him for teaching me about the importance of the small things.

He practiced in California for years before coming to Texas. When he set up in the Lone Star State, he started doing some house calls by happenstance. It wasn't his main business plan, just one strategy for growing his clinic. It didn't take long for him to realize, "Why am I focusing on clinic work when the house-call side of the business is underserved?" No one else was doing it. It was a niche within a niche.

That our paths crossed was remarkable. It all started when he was at a seminar out west. In line for lunch, he started chatting with people around him. He was extremely outgoing that way. The woman standing in front of him asked where he was from, and he said, "Houston, Texas." Then she asked him what he did for a living. After he answered, she said, "No way! I have a cousin that also lives in Houston and is a podiatrist. Small world." It turned out that *I* was her cousin podiatrist. They exchanged information, and then he got into contact with me.

As I was starting my practice from scratch, he hired me to do house calls for him. At that time, he was at the end of his career. Some things prohibited him physically, so he needed somebody like me to handle some of his house calls.

If we were together doing house calls, we'd go to lunch. Most of the time it was his favorite taco place. It was the kind of restaurant that gave you chips and salsa first, giving you a few minutes to talk and go over things before your meal came out.

On one of the most impactful days of my life, he told me something that changed the trajectory of my career. "You know," he said, "I'm sure that money could be made in surgery. But surgeries take time. You have to show up at the center, see the patient and family, get cleaned and cleared from the previous surgery, do the potentially hours-long surgery, and then stay married to that patient for the ninety-day global period." For those unaware, that global period means doctors are obligated to treat the patient for free if anything happens after the surgery.

He continued, "In a morning when someone can knock out one or two surgeries, I could go see fifteen patients, check their feet, clip their toenails, and make twice as much." There it was…the value of the bread and the butter.

He helped me understand that it's not about doing the biggest, most glamorous thing. With that said, if you're good at the glamorous thing and do it better than everyone else, great. But the principle Dr. Anthon instilled in me is that the small, simple, overlooked, and under-appreciated things can be leveraged.

Those foundational things, when done well, can turn into big things.

BUILDING A BUSINESS FOUNDATION

So far, I've been weaving bread and butter, Michael Jordan, and fungal toenails all together. Food, basketball, and podiatry each have their own sets of fundamentals. It follows then that there are fundamentals for everything. With that in mind, it's now important to acknowledge that we are actually embedded in multiple disciplines. For example, I'm not only a podiatrist but also a business owner. Yet, I never went to business school. Unless you majored in business or got an MBA, the same is likely true for you, too.

What does this tell us? If we want to be professionally successful, one pathway is to master the fundamentals of our unique trade *and* how to run a business. That's what I decided to do: to make a go of it and learn business administration as best I could.

Doctors tend not to get formal business training because, first and foremost, we are spending that time studying medicine. But it's also because there's an expectation that doctors take a job with a hospital, large group, or other healthcare company that is already administrating the business. That's just the Darwinism of medical businesses as it has evolved over the decades.

Doctors are so seldom involved in the business side of healthcare that, in the last sixty years or so, the number of healthcare administrators has skyrocketed relative to the number of doctors.

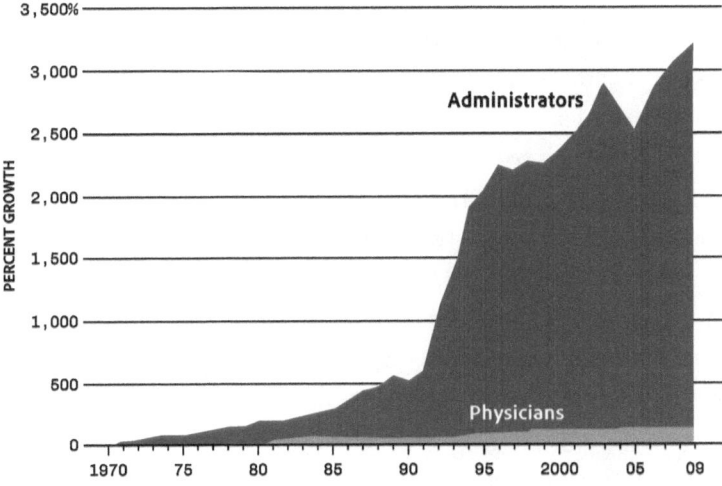

GROWTH IN PHYSICIANS AND ADMINISTRATORS

Part of this jump is the result of healthcare becoming a complicated and highly regulated industry. Healthcare business administration has even become an expertise unto itself—many places of education now offering their own degrees in the field. That's why, these days, most doctors don't start their own practice until they've worked for three to five years to generate enough business experience.

And even fewer doctors leave residency on a Friday and, on Monday, have their own business open to see patients, generate claims, bill, and start to bring revenue. But that's what I did.

It was thanks to a one-hour lecture I went to in my last year of med school. I repeat: one hour. That's how much business training was made available to us. And it was voluntary. But that one hour made my next few decades possible. (That might be a literal example of finding value in a small thing.) The doctor who ran the seminar visited my Ohio campus and ended up being from Houston. Later he would become a mentor.

The goal of the seminar was to prepare doctors for opening their own practice after that standard period of time: three to five years after entering the workforce. Despite that, I wanted to start right after my residency. I wanted to be like my father, who had always owned his own dental practice.

One of the tools that he gave us was an example business plan. I looked at that plan like it was a secret treasure map. It was so detailed, it even listed the cost of Band-Aids. It talked about subleases, tenant-improvement allowances, and medical equipment leasing options. It helped me study reimbursement codes, billable amounts, expected payments, and cited marketing plans. *This is huge*, I thought when I first saw it. It was like a gift.

I still had three years of residency before I'd be out in the workforce, so I'd have plenty of time to get into every nook and cranny of the example business plan while prepping my own. Using it as a map to chart my own path became a three-year expedition. I put together market research, proformas, and organizational models of similar businesses. I'd tinker away on it when I had the time.

Flash-forward a few years, and at the beginning of my last year of residency, I had this robust business plan. It was organized and written to be coherent for investors and banks instead of other doctors. And I was proud of it.

About nine months before graduation, I went to secure a $75,000 loan from a local bank with my business plan under my arm. I spent twenty dollars to wrap it in a padfolio to make it look nice. I put in tabs for ease of navigation. The whole nine yards.

As I walked in, I was greeted by Annie—my banker who, later, became a very good friend of mine. She ushered me into one of those conference rooms with the frosted glass walls.

After introductions, I put my leather-bound business plan on the table in front of her. I didn't need it anymore; I had memorized everything and had internalized my presentation, my pitch. And so I told her about my aspirations and what I wanted to do with my business plan.

I also had an ace up my sleeve: additional income from working with Dr. Anthon. That provided a cushion to offset the initial startup costs and working capital so I could make my monthly payments. It reduced the bank's risks.

After I was done, there was silence. I was a bit worried. And then she spoke. "In all of the years I've worked here and with all of the big companies that look to work with us, I have never seen anything as complete as this." That's when she told me she wanted to set up a second meeting with the regional vice president of commercial banking. His name was Chris.

So I went to this second meeting, sat down with Chris, and went through my whole spiel again. He said the same thing: "I've never seen a business plan like this, and certainly not from somebody who's never had a business before. This is a fantastic plan."

Off he went to talk to the underwriters and the lenders, the folks in charge of crunching the numbers to see if a given investment is viable for the bank. When we heard back from the underwriters, they weren't quite as impressed. Their conclusion was, quite flatly, no. The major concern was that I had no business experience. And I hadn't even graduated residency. They weren't wrong.

I wouldn't say I was surprised, but I was disappointed. Annie and Chris broke the news to me, but they weren't kicking me out just yet.

Because I demonstrated foundational skills with my business plan, they told me that they believed in me. They hatched a plan to go back and reverse the decision. First they went to the underwriters. Then they went to the VPs. Annie told me at a later meeting, "We went to bat for you. We told them that we fully trust you and are confident in you." After that, Annie gave me a $50,000 line of credit.

That amount carried me for six years in my practice. And that gave me the ability to grow my practice into a thriving clinic. From my practice's income, I was able to open two more clinics and also buy Dr. Anthon's a few short years later.

It wasn't until later, when I bought a company that was substantially more valuable than anything I had before, that I went back to Annie. I asked for a $100,000 line of credit. They offered me $250,000.

In the business world, the business plan is the bread and butter. Every startup needs one. Without it, nobody will believe in you and, more importantly, nobody will invest in you. So, if you're looking to run your own business, that means you won't have the opportunity to utilize your training and expertise to make a living, let alone find success. And for many people who are experts in something other than business, a business plan is easily overlooked. But never overlook the fundamentals.

Thankfully, I didn't overlook it. In fact, I did the opposite. I practiced and mastered that fundamental element of business, and it made all the difference. A one-hour seminar turned into three years of toil that made my next two decades possible.

Sometimes, starting small and finding value in that underserved or unglamorous work can create big, life-changing consequences.

DO WHAT FEW OTHERS DO

To exemplify how finding an underserved niche can lead to success, I want to talk about Madam C.J. Walker. She was the first American self-made female millionaire, born into slavery but left the world wealthy. When I think of finding success by finding an underserved niche and doing what few others do, she is one of the first that comes to my mind.

What makes her story so unique? Walker earned her fortune and built a business empire by recognizing an underserved market: Black women's hair-care products. When she opened her business in 1906, very few companies offered products or services that specifically catered to Black customers.

Prior to that, she began to lose her hair. Over time, she observed that many other Black women were experiencing the same or similar hair loss issues. That's when she saw a need for products specifically designed for Black women. Turning toward her inventive and innovative skills, she experimented with different ingredients—coconut oil, beeswax, copper sulfate, and sulfur, to create a scalp preparation, ointment, iron comb, and shampoo—to combine and act as treatment for the issue she and many other women faced. Courageously, she tested her experimental products on herself until she found one that helped her hair grow back.

For a while, she sold her product door-to-door. Then she started Madam C.J. Walker Manufacturing Company, which specialized in cosmetics and hair-care products for Black women. The products themselves were effective, but they also succeeded because she did what others weren't doing at the time, including emphasizing women's health and creating and selling directly to Black women.

She then hired thousands of women, which in turn helped many gain financial independence through career opportunities. As she grew her empire, she saw a need for salons that catered to Black women, so she opened several, still built on the same foundational knowledge she cultivated earlier. She even started a beauty school to help women learn the skills required to work in the salons. In a brilliant moment of early brand synergy, she made sure to supply those salons with her own hair-care products.

Walker's success wasn't just about selling a product and attaining financial wealth; it was about identifying an opportunity that others ignored and building on fundamentals of business to pave a new path for future entrepreneurs. She did what few others were doing. And she did it well.

FINDING VALUE IN THE UNDERAPPRECIATED THINGS

Here's another inspiring story.

Picture this. You're cleaning dishes and toilets at Denny's during off-hours. Your elbow strains as you grip the brush and swirl it around the porcelain. Drops of your sweat fall into the bowl and ripple the surface of the toilet water. Thankfully, it's the last thing you'll have to clean up tonight, the last object covered in the bile and debris of the restaurant's customers.

The bathroom is clean. The kitchen is immaculate. You're exhausted. And you've spent eight minimum-wage hours in the middle of the night in the throes of difficult labor while inhaling the burning scent of cleaning chemicals. For all of that hard work, you'll earn $58, or around $46 after taxes.

What I've just described to you was a typical night in the young life of Jensen Huang, the current CEO of NVIDIA. At the time of writing, the company he runs is worth $3.5 trillion. Whether speaking in person or giving an interview, he lauds his Denny's job as being the experience that instilled in him humility, a strong work ethic, and attention to detail. Huang has emphasized that it taught him that there was no task beneath him. The underappreciated things are part of a successful enterprise. He once humorously told an audience of tech workers, "I've cleaned more toilets than all of you combined, and some of them I just can't unsee."

I'll talk about the importance of hard work and effort in a future chapter. But right now, I'm most interested in the humility he learned that helps a person stay attuned to detail. Those skills helped him understand that *all* parts of an organization have fundamental traits required to make the whole thing succeed. He even refers to Denny's as his "alma mater."

For him, the smallest gig was part of his path to something much bigger. He built a path on that foundation. And that path was cleared by him finding value in small things that most would find too unglamorous to seek out.

Small things are like LEGO blocks. Just one isn't particularly spectacular. But when you start stacking them on top of each other, something wonderful can happen.

A fantastic example of this is how ancient horses directly and incrementally, over the millenia, influenced the design of rocket ships.

When two horses are standing side by side, the distance across them is roughly four feet, eight inches. Why two horses? Because ancient Egyptians and Sumerians, after first using vehicles pulled by one horse, realized that two-horsed vehicles could pull the most efficient and cost effective. Two horses became the standard, and vehicle axles were made at four feet, eight inches.

Later, when Romans developed their own chariots and modes of transportation, they copied the ancient Egyptians and Sumerians. Shortly afterward, Romans then conquered much of the Mediterranean world. As they expanded outward, they needed to connect the empire with a road system. Those roads needed to accommodate vehicles that were four feet, eight inches wide. So that's the size that each lane of the road became, those lanes meant to allow travel in opposite directions like a modern road.

Those Roman roads reached as far north as the UK. Then, during the medieval period, when England designed their wagons and carts, they engineered their vehicle sizes based on the Roman roads. As time went on, British roadways were standardized based on these ancient Roman practices. And then the British railroad gauge was determined by their pre-established road size.

Meanwhile, in America, many of the early US rail systems were built by British engineers. Even today, the standard lane and railway size is four feet, eight inches.

In the twentieth century, when NASA started designing the space shuttle, there was a limitation to consider: Rocket ship components would have to be manufactured elsewhere and delivered via America's railways system, which was based on the British system.

The tunnels and tracks constrained the maximum diameter of the rocket boosters that needed to lift the craft off the tarmac. In the end, rocket boosters were indirectly limited by the American railroad gauge that was based on the British railways, which itself was based on Roman roads, whose roads were sized by ancient chariots, those chariots designed to be the width of two horses' butts.

What's amazing is that this chain is linked with thousands of years of one little thing leading to the next. It's littered with the slow buildup of fundamental, underappreciated things. And it ends with a rocket, one of the most advanced forms of technology created. Without the bread and the butter, rocket ships would not be possible.

From horses to rockets. From earth to the stars. Little things, when harnessed, can act as the foundation of something much bigger and more powerful. In our own lives, we can carefully and mindfully leverage the value of small things to make the success we define for ourselves.

I started with a one-hour seminar on how to open up a practice. That led to a leather-bound notebook filled with the pages of my business plan. The book opened the door to a bank, which invested in me. That money opened the door for my first, small practice. Within that niche of podiatry I focused on another small thing: clipping toenails, a common but underserved aspect of my profession...or the bread and butter of podiatry. From the revenue that little business generated, I added three more practices. And now where is it? Following the links in the chain, I currently help Allevio serve dozens of podiatrists all across the country, providing expert tools and solutions to help podiatry practices thrive.

In order to build something on a solid foundation, it's going to take getting your hands dirty in a not-so-glamorous way. You'll have to grind. And there's going to be adversity. But if you stick with it, you'll come out the other end of that storm with a reward.

CHAPTER 2

EMBRACING THE GRIND

"Opportunity is missed by most people because it is dressed in overalls and looks like work."

—THOMAS EDISON

I should have died.

Maybe part of me did die, because I would never be the same afterward. It was Super Bowl weekend in 2015, and I was on a snowmobile trip with my close friends.

The last thing I remember was flying through the air, looking down at the tops of trees as they passed by underneath me. It was majestic and terrifying.

Sometime later, and with a gasp, I woke up in the snow. Shards of plastic from the visor of my helmet were lodged into my face and scattered all around me. Snow had piled into my visor and around my face, and I struggled to breathe. I tried to reach with my hands to start pulling myself out, and that's when I realized…I couldn't move.

I was completely paralyzed.

Sensing my body position, I could tell I was upside down. For what seemed like a long time, I shouted "Help!" as loud as I could. It was like shouting into a void. Then the combination of semiconsciousness, disorientation, and suffocation sent me into a panic. *God, please save me*, I prayed.

Pretty quickly, that panic transformed into a feeling I hadn't felt before or experienced since: dread. It was the dread of knowing that, quite probably, I would die. There I was, encased in snow, all alone, unable to move, and unable to say "goodbye" and "I love you" to my wife and children one last time.

DISSOLVE LIKE SNOW

The lead-up to my snowmobile accident started a month earlier.

My professional life, at that time, was undergoing a lot of exceptional changes. The management company had just transferred all management duties back to me. I added more employees, including my first associate. We were growing so quickly that we had recently switched our practice management software from a basic, free version to a paid, high-quality version to accommodate that growth.

The practice was less than a month removed from relocation. We upgraded from a closet-sized space that was subleased to our very own two-thousand-square-foot, modern clinic space. It had a private office for me in a corner that overlooked the neighboring hospital. For all intents and purposes, prior to leaving on my snowmobile trip, I had arrived professionally.

And my personal life was no different. My wife and I had welcomed our third child. We were in the process of building our dream home. And when we put the home we were living in on the market, the major feedback we got from prospective buyers was that the house was very "lived in." In real estate terms, that is not a description you want for your house. But it meant that we spent all kinds of time together there. The drywall dings, baseboard scratches, and other remnants of our love was evidenced in our "lived in" home.

I was in the midst of living an amazing life.

In that spirit, and at the start of a new year, my father-in-law and I decided to plan a Super Bowl weekend trip with some of my closest friends and some of his closest friends. There would be about twelve of us. And the goal was to spend time at our family cabin in Heber City, Utah—a remote spot in Park City near mountainous landscapes of majestic snow.

We arrived on a Wednesday night in February. Right off the bat, we went and picked up our snowmobile rentals to kick off the weekend's adventures. That adventure would begin the next day, as the first night was for breaking bread and celebrating our excitement to be able to get together for the weekend.

Thursday morning rolled around quickly. Getting ready was quite the sight. There were a bunch of Texas guys trying to figure out how to bundle in cold-weather clothes. We had to buy these foreign garments shortly after we landed. Like fish out of water, we were out of our element.

My father-in-law was the most experienced one in the group. So after breakfast he went over the safety procedures. *Here's how to start the snowmobile. This is how you shut it down. Here's how to operate it safely. Here's the emergency brake. Keep a compass on you, as well as a flashlight. And don't forget an extra set of batteries. If you lose the ignition key, the extra is stored in this compartment. Keep an eye out for ice. Here are the signs of an avalanche, so stay sharp.*

He went through everything.

Afterward, we set off. As the group drove out to start the

day, my snowmobile was having a little difficulty for the first two hundred yards or so. Then, all of a sudden, a pop of flame screeched out of my sled and caught my right pant leg on fire.

In teaching our group how to use the sled, my father-in-law had left the emergency brake on. Whoops! Thankfully, there was enough snow around where I could calmly step off and put out the fire. After inspecting my sled a little more, it was deemed safe to drive.

Looking back, that moment should have been the sign that told me I should have probably stayed at the cabin. A reasonable person would have said something like, "Alright, well this is probably not a good idea. Maybe the fire is a warning sign." But I persisted.

It will be fine, I thought.

The day unfolded, and we had a great time in the mountains going up and down big basin bowls of nature. It was ten thousand acres of pure American majesty. Extremely remote. No cell signal. Just us and the world.

It was getting late, so about half of us started back toward the cabin. We had a challenge on our hands. As the sun starts going down and the temperature drops a little, you get what's called gray mist. It's this phenomenon where the sky and snow become the same color and, unfortunately for me, indistinguishable. Just a blanket of gray. In those conditions, there's no way to see much of the topography that you're driving over.

Initially, I was leading the charge home. But, being the fun-seeker that I am, I was able to spot a few little hills that would be a great nightcap to the day's work. So I broke off. Because of the gray mist, I became dramatically separated from the group.

I wasn't concerned. I was enjoying the ride. Right about then is when, at full speed, I launched myself off a cliff. Thanks to the gray mist, the twenty-five-foot drop-off became visible just as my sled's skis passed over it.

I looked down, and I saw the trees pass below me.

After I woke up and my situation was becoming clearer to me, I knew my friends were nowhere close. How could they be? I got who-knows-how-far from them and then fell twenty-five feet in zero visibility. It was unlikely they'd think I ended up down here, let alone be able to find the "down here" I ended up in.

When the dread of death washed over me, one small part of my rational brain was still working. My death, I assumed, would likely result from hypothermia as a consequence of being unable to lift myself out of the snow. I didn't know the extent of my injuries, but there was also a small chance, I realized, that those injuries could end me before hypothermia, especially if I was bleeding out.

What happened next was nothing short of a miracle.

Still on their trek back to the cabin, one of my closest friends, Jake, stopped in his tracks. Later he would tell me that he did it all of a sudden and for no real reason—like his sled was hitting an invisible wall. He just had this feeling. Flagging down Steve, another friend of ours, Jake blurted out, "We have to go find Marcin!"

Steve almost talked Jake down, preventing the search party. But, when he saw Jake's eyes, he saw a look he never forgot. Steve immediately knew something was wrong. I'm forever grateful for whatever feeling Jake had, because if Steve didn't experience the fear on Jake's face, I'd probably be dead.

The miraculous continued. The ravine where I ended up couldn't really be identified unless somebody was looking down over the edge. That's exactly what they did. The flipped and in-pieces yellow snowmobile contrasted with the gray mist of the snow down below. If my snowmobile wasn't yellow, they never would've seen it or me.

They hobbled down the cliff face, and they described me as looking like I had been shot into the snow like an arrow. My feet were sticking straight up out of the snow, the snow itself covering me up to my thigh. As they got closer, Jake experienced one of the most horrible sounds he'd ever heard: my muffled screams.

They started digging me out. When they got the leverage, they pulled me out of the snow and rolled me over. The first thing I said was, "Steve! What are you doing in Utah?!" Apparently I kept asking that every few minutes for the next few hours. It was clear to them, in my disorientation, that I had suffered a concussion. Then I told them I couldn't move my arms or legs.

Shortly after, a couple more people from our group showed up. They started strategizing. We were in ten thousand acres of remote gray mist with no cell signal, and none of us knew from this location how to get back to the cabin. In order to get back, somebody would have to track down my father-in-law so that we knew where we were going. Two left to find my father-in-law.

Lying down was unbearably painful for me. As we waited, my friends Joe and Jimmy sat upright behind me and took turns leaning their backs against mine. They literally had my back. I was so grateful. It allowed me to sit upright and lessen the pain. There we sat for forty-five minutes.

I remember sitting there and looking at my legs, trying to make them move. They wouldn't.

Shock and delirium were my primary experience at that time. It didn't provide me much opportunity to think about the reality of being paralyzed. But I remember being so grateful that I was alive and that I'd be able to see my family again.

After that, I remember looking down at my hands. They had been placed against my chest and balled into fists. They weren't moving either. A sense of terror washed over me. As a doctor who clips toenails for a living and who performs surgery, I needed my hands to support my family.

These moments of reflection were brief. Because of my head injury, I would quickly shift focus and feel a great sense of surprise to see Steve. "Steve! What are you doing in Utah?!"

We waited for our friends to return with my father-in-law, but they never found him. Instead, somehow, in the ongoing miracle that was this day, they came across two avid snowmobilers from Florida, not a place where they could pursue their hobby locally. They had a cabin nearby that had a cell signal. So my friends followed the Floridians back to their cabin.

The moment they arrived, they dialed 911. The operator inquired about my location. My friends were from Texas, so all they could muster was, "It's in an area called 'Timberlakes.'" It was a huge area, one too big for a rescue unit to find anything quickly.

Another miracle was stacked onto the previous ones. It just so happened that the operator received a similar phone call a week earlier. He suspected that I had driven off the same cliff in that area.

Lo and behold, the Life Flight Network helicopter found us. All of my friends carried me up and out of the ravine on one of those medical boards. They handed me over to the paramedics, which gave me an overwhelming sense of calmness.

One of the paramedics asked, "Do you have your phone? Let me know if I can call your wife or family." He called my wife. She picked up, and the paramedic told her about the accident, that I was okay and alive, and that I was on my way to the hospital.

I could hear her yelling at this poor guy. Phrases like "I'm not falling for this!" and "You guys can't prank me!" By the time we arrived at the hospital, we had to call her a few more times before she'd stay on the phone long enough to hear us out. Then *I* got on the phone. When it finally clicked with her and she knew it was serious, she let me have it: "How could you be so stupid?!" I'll never forget her saying that. Good spouses like my wife, above all else, want us to be the best versions of ourselves and, just as importantly, want us around.

My life almost dissolved like snow. It was a close call, but thankfully my story continued. And once I had been saved, that's when the real work began.

THE LONG ROAD TO BETTERMENT

After the doctors got done with their assessment, I had six broken ribs, nine broken vertebrae, and a chunk of my spinal column lodged in my spinal cord. A fragment of bone from my C5 was lodged in my C6 vertebrae. It should be noted that those innervate the hands, tools I needed as a physician. Feeling in my legs returned about an hour later, which was extremely reassuring. But it would be days before I could move my hands.

In the ICU for a few weeks, time passed impossibly slowly and impossibly quickly at the same time. It was one of those periods of life where it's tough to remember most of the details. People visited me that I can't remember ever seeing.

I do remember waking up one day to see my oldest brother, Ryan, at my bedside. He had always taken good care of me growing up. He flew out immediately and stayed by my side for weeks.

After my wife and I found childcare, she flew out. She was

overwhelmed with the response of our friends and neighbors. They all pitched in to watch our kids so that she could be with me.

The abundance of support allowed me to reflect more deeply on what had just happened and what I faced moving forward. My practice was only two years old. I had just taken giant leaps forward—big risks—to try and grow my business. It was the start of the year, and I had just switched my insurance to a $10,000 out-of-pocket max because I wasn't expecting any major health concerns at that age. And it didn't cover the helicopter ride, which was $140,000.

It all added up to the thought that I would lose my business. All that time, effort, and energy in my education, in my residency, and in developing my business plan could, seemingly, have been for nothing. But my determination wouldn't let that happen.

In order to regain the use of my hands and feet, I needed C5-C6 fusion surgery. The procedure was successful. Afterwards, I stayed in the hospital in Utah for several more weeks. The rehabilitation portion lasted six weeks. There, they had me complete long regiments of breathing and physical therapy. When I returned home, I couldn't leave the house and had to do an additional six weeks of physical therapy. It wasn't especially difficult, but it was intensive and regular. It was a grind, and it was ugly.

Moreover, it was a commitment. It was a fight for survival. It was a fight to thrive again. When I did recover, I continued to practice. I regained and maintained full functionality using my hands. I can continue to play the guitar and other instruments. I can draw. I can fletch a bow. I can hold my children. And I can clip toenails better than anybody.

My snowmobile accident was like drawing back a compound bow. In order to propel the arrow forward, you first have to strain to pull it back and put it in the right position. It takes hard work before you're ready to launch forward. My accident was a setback, to be sure. But it was also an opportunity. When faced with the need to work hard toward recovery and betterment, the choice is always to work hard. To grind. Two steps backward to get three steps forward. My recovery was going to become whatever I made it. To see the rainbow, I had to get through the storm.

As I exited that experience and put it behind me, I came out of it with zero remorse, regret, resentment, or anger for it happening. But it changed me. I've never done anything the same after my accident. It influences every decision I make.

Even in the absolute worst circumstances, there are things you can learn. There are things that will benefit you.

THE BUTTON THAT ALWAYS WORKED

The first Sunday I was able to go back to church after my accident, my friend Steve—the one who agreed to go look for me with Jake—got up to talk to the congregation. He's a pilot by trade. He told this story about a button in the cockpit of a plane. When pressed, it would function to help land the plane.

In his thousands and thousands of hours in flight, that button had always worked to do what it was supposed to do. He never worried about it—there was no reason to worry. He would always reach up, push the button, and the functioning button would help land the plane. Always.

During one of his flights across the country, he reached up and pushed the button. It didn't work. A short panic set over him; it had never not worked before. What would he do? How could he land the plane? The way he normally landed a plane was now off the table. Thankfully, his extensive training kicked back in and he was able to safely land the plane manually.

It dawned on him that he had taken that button for granted. He relied so heavily on that button. He'd push it and get a response. Push it. Response. Push it. Response. Push it. Response. And so on and so on.

After that landing experience, he never pushed that button again without being grateful for it and mindful of what purpose it had. He had to rethink how he viewed that button. It was now his safety net, and he'd remember that he could land the plane without it. Going through that difficult process ended up benefitting his pilot skillset—staying sharp and keeping an active mindset during flight.

We almost didn't make it to church to hear his story that day. Our kids were kind of protesting it. They were all young—within the realm of toddler-meltdown age. It was one of those moments that many parents experience with young kids. It's easy to lose control, everybody's emotions get bigger, and it's tough. I remember that *I* didn't even want to go with that morning being so difficult. I felt short-tempered, angry that my kids were being so difficult.

But there I sat, listening to my friend who had saved my life on the side of a mountain. I looked back at my kids and thought, *I can never take them for granted like that button*. I could have easily died on that mountain, never getting to experience Sunday morning meltdowns again. I realized at that moment that we can underappreciate things until we don't have them. I sat there and reflected on my accident and Steve's story. That's when I decided to appreciate every second of my life, my family, and every interaction I have with them.

Setbacks are setbacks. There's no doubt about it. They are hard. They are difficult. They are usually unwelcome. In addition to those things, and to reiterate for emphasis, they are a source of opportunity. There's not a single day that goes by that I don't implement something I gained from my accident. Perhaps most profoundly, my accident and John's reliance on the button in his cockpit help us refocus on what we can be grateful for.

Our lives are filled with buttons like these—things we don't appreciate until the moment we don't have them.

I worked countless hours for several weeks to regain the function in my hands and feet. It was a grind. But I was grateful for a work ethic that helped me get to where I knew I wanted to be. In the end, going through something difficult can actually be to your benefit. It can make you better. Challenges make you who you are.

THE COMPOUND BOW

There's a huge difference between failure—or mistakes—and the grind. The grind is the unglamorous, tough work. It's getting deep into the dirty work that acts as motivational challenges.

The challenges themselves make you who you are. In my experience, sticking with the grind can increase your chances of success. You can make yourself into a diamond from the pressure and heat of daily work, of daily difficulties that are the source of opportunity.

And best of all, you can make the grind what you want. That's why I hesitate to call my recovery "tough" or "difficult." I wholeheartedly wanted to get back to where I was. That determination and resilience ensured that, in no uncertain terms, I didn't view my rehab as difficult. It wasn't difficult. It was necessary. If I let myself view it as hard, maybe I would have been less inclined to push through.

Now, I'm not saying you need a full-on mindset shift like that. I simply want to point out that we can, to some extent, make the unique grind that we each face whatever we want it to become. If we view it as difficult, don't be surprised when it starts getting more difficult. If we view it as necessary and take it one step at a time, we'll be on to greener pastures before we know it. That's my philosophy.

When trials arrive, big or small, *you* have a choice. You can let them control you or you can welcome them to overcome them. When you approach it from the latter perspective, challenges don't become any less difficult but you become much more capable.

Most of the time, the grind doesn't require overcoming spinal fusion surgery. For most of us, including me, it might be consistently doing our accounting. Challenges are challenges. All of it is dirty work. The unglamorous, routine, daily, essential things that can set us apart to help us find success. It's clipping toenails, driving a garbage truck, sorting items in a warehouse, cleaning a crime scene, delivering food, or anything else.

Regardless of what you do, in order to do it to your highest potential, you'll face a tough grind. You'll take two steps back before you can go three steps forward.

It reminds me of when I witnessed the power of a compound bow. I learned how to shoot a bow with my brother, Ryan. Now Ryan is also a doctor like me, but you might not notice that when you first meet him. He likes to wear overalls and go catfish noodling in Oklahoma. If you ran into him outside of his professional career, you might mistake him for a farmer, not a doctor. In other words, I was in good hands when learning from him.

What surprised me the most about the process was how

hard it is to pull back the strings of a compound bow. I witnessed a compound bow's power during a training for youth. The man in charge of the training really wanted to hammer home how hard using a compound bow was. So he invited anyone who thought they were strong enough to come up and pull the bow back.

That's when all of these high-school-aged boys started clamoring to be the first person up there to impress the crowd. Of course, the first three or four couldn't pull it back at all. Then one kid could kind of move it back a little bit. Finally a big football lineman kid saunters up there, pretty confident. He did get it back, but you could see the tremor and shake in his arm.

Then he called up a specific kid for a demonstration. He was pretty scrawny, and superficially one would assume that he'd struggle like the other kids did. But the moment he put his hand on the bow, everybody could tell that he knew what he was doing. His left hand found a consciously chosen part of the bow, which he then pointed to the ground. When he drew his arm, it was clear that he was thoughtfully squeezing his shoulder blades together, locking his hips, and flexing out his chest. The string easily and uniformly rested against his cheek, and he stood there like a statue. What was extremely difficult for others, with regular practice and resilience, was easy for another.

The speaker congratulated the young man and sent him back to his seat. Then he made some observations for all of us to reflect on. By gripping and manipulating the bow in a certain way, pulling the string back can be an easier strain on the body. And when the string is pulled back, it can send a projectile significantly farther, much faster, and with more force than a regular bow. That's because the string on the bow, when taken back in a specific manner, actually generates the force required to shoot it hundreds of yards.

There are many times in life when we want to shoot ourselves forward, to go into the world and find immediate progress. But in order to do that, we must first draw backward to generate the force required to go forward. It takes power and steadiness to pull the string backward, hold it there, and track the center of the target. Backward motion is required before forward motion.

And it can get dirty. Think about wounds. It's part of the grind in medicine. The wound, by its very nature, produces all kinds of gunk. If you want that wound to heal well and have skin grow back, you have to scrape the gunk off. Not only is that a messy process, but it actually makes the wound a little bigger and deeper. It has to get a little bit worse before it can get better. Two steps backward, three steps forward. It's a challenge filled with a pressure that will push back against your progress.

But the tension—that pressure—is the daily grind of dirty, ugly work. It could be work during despair or recovering from a catastrophic event. It could be anything you deem a challenge. Regardless, that challenge is an opportunity.

What might feel like something difficult—being drawn back—might actually be you on the brink of launching forward.

OF CHICKEN AND GRITS

That process of drawing back to launch forward is—or should be—a cyclical process. One of the misconceptions about success is that if a person does X, Y, and Z, they'll be instantly successful. But it actually requires resilience, perseverance, hard work, and repeatedly learning from experience. For many people, that might not result in success until later.

In terms of "late bloomers," consider that Colonel Sanders earned his wealth at the ripe age of sixty-two years old. Yes, he had started his famous Kentucky Fried Chicken restaurant when he was forty, but his single restaurant occupied a hole-in-the-wall gas station in the middle of nowhere. It took decades of hard work building up his food's reputation, smartly protecting his now-famous recipe, and gaining enough capital to open several restaurants that gave him the leverage to sell franchising rights. But that decades-long journey wasn't the only grit the colonel displayed. What's the plural of grit? Is it grits? Whatever it is, it paired nicely with the colonel's chicken.

Before starting KFC, he worked a series of odd jobs. He was a steamboat pilot, which checks out. He is exactly what I imagine a steamboat pilot to look like. But he was also an insurance salesman, a farmer, a streetcar conductor, and a fireman. These trades, while many were likely stopgaps to help him make a living along the way, were nonetheless contributors to his restaurant success. They taught him a variety of skills and were part of his grind to see the rainbow through the rain.

For example, he used his insurance salesman skills to knock on restaurant and store doors to pitch his idea for KFC. He faced more than a thousand rejections before securing the aforementioned space in the gas station. During that time, he slept in his car and faced steep challenges. His success story wasn't about age or luck. He persevered and maintained an attitude of relentless hard work—of embracing the grind—until he saw financial success.

THE GRIND WORKS

It was the first time that my current company, Allevio, bought a clinic outside of my group. We purchased it from somebody who had worked for me before. I would keep in touch with him every few months just to see how he was doing and to make sure everything was okay.

After about six years, we lost touch. When I did reach back out to him, he revealed to me that he was actually going to lose his practice. Apparently it wasn't making money and, since this was during the COVID-19 pandemic, it was actually costing him money. He was having to take loans just to keep it open.

He considered moving somewhere else to try again, but he also thought about possibly just taking another job at somebody else's practice.

Minutes after I got off the phone with him, I had a meeting with my expansion and marketing team. They presented a list of names of doctors in the area that would be potential fits for us. Remarkably, his name was at the top of the list. So I called him back and asked him not to sell his practice and move just yet. "Let me see if we can come in and help you."

"But," I added, "things will get worse before they get better." We changed everything. His records system, workflow, how his patients were roomed, front desk communications, marketing strategies, billing and collections…everything. Obviously, the purpose was to improve everything, but because everything was new, there were some setbacks as well as a major learning curve. At one point, the front desk communication system went down for hours at a time. Compensation wasn't distributed on time in one instance. (Not paying people on time, as you can imagine, generates a major blow to team culture and morale.)

My friend was in the midst of the grind. Not only was his routine interrupted by the necessary work of learning many new systems, he also had to put out a bunch of fires (mistakes) that come with making changes. He had to keep seeing patients, keep offering them high-quality care, and keep generating revenue despite these setbacks on the business side of the clinic.

The grind, it turns out, often includes taking steps backward before forward progress can be made. He'd have to learn new things, adapt, implement changes, be steadfast in new routines, and be resilient if the goal was to make this practice thrive. He kept his gears spinning and grinding. He went from a diesel engine that starts up with those horrible coughing and sputtering noises to a well-oiled machine.

We ended up paying off all his practice's debt and assumed ownership. After implementing our strategies in our partnership, his practice now carries three doctors and has doubled its revenue, all within three months of work. Soon, his clinic was breaking records and has become one of our best. In one month, they now produce the same revenue that they used to produce annually.

The grind works. Putting your head down and doing the dirty, routine, and difficult work has a huge impact on how far you can fly.

What's fascinating about this fact is that, generally speaking, we're not taught to value the dirty work. What I experienced in my medical training, I believe, is somewhat universal to any profession. The unglamorous work is seen as something beneath us. Hard work is seen as less important, and that often leads to unfair stereotypes.

You often hear things like, "You'll end up being a burger flipper," as if hard work in the kitchen of the food service industry is something to scoff at. This type of thinking follows all sorts of unglamorous things, like driving a garbage truck or clipping toenails.

That dirty work is often labeled as a punishment. Residency

as a podiatrist, for example, is much like any profession. You have to learn the trade by starting at the bottom rung. For us, being at the bottom comes after four years in postgraduate medical school, including monthlong externships at residency programs. But placement as an extern is no guarantee of becoming a resident; the program will show interest in everyone so they are considered a "desirable" residency. As a first-year resident, you start all over as the low man on the totem pole. In my situation, we worked hundred-hour weeks. I slept *at* the hospital countless times. (My secret was getting a room in the maternity ward. They have more comfortable beds and nicer bathrooms.) Even though I was a podiatry resident, most of our work was what everyone else preferred not to do. So, in my time, I did a lot of proctology, urology surgeries, and somewhere around one hundred vaginal hysterectomies...as a foot doctor.

Residents are kind of the minions of the attending physicians. You're at their beck and call, and you can never do things right. If there is blame to be handed out, it's usually pinned on a resident. I've seen surgeons throw instruments across the operating room when they nick a blood vessel and blame the resident standing on the other side of the room! That kind of environment teaches you resilience. It teaches you to buck up, get tough, get your hands dirty, and get used to that routine of challenging work.

For many people in this sort of pipeline, the thinking is that, one day, you'll rise above that hard work and "make it" by doing ten big surgeries a day while making a bajillion dollars. The attending physicians were meant to be evidence of that for us; they were these ultra-experienced almost-gods who had made it. I've seen these kinds of doctors do lots of big, complicated surgical procedures. Everything you can think of, simple to complex. We were meant to be in awe of them and want to replicate their careers with our own. Most of my residency colleagues set that as their path to success.

These supposedly successful doctors also tended to have a negative outlook on other podiatrists who clipped toenails. It was "beneath them." They felt elevated above anybody willing to make the dirty work part of their overarching mission or career. I've heard respected surgeons talk about "toenail clipper" podiatrists as people who are stuck clipping toenails because they aren't good at surgery. *Not* doing complex, reconstructive surgery must have been a career concession.

Through it all, these surgeons—some of whom I greatly respect for their fantastic work—didn't recognize the value of the bread and butter. To them, the only thing to do was the glamorous thing. If all that you have is a hammer, everything you see is a nail. Some tended to push surgical options on patients prematurely under the notion that the more time you spent in the operating room meant that you sat higher on the throne!

Thankfully, I found myself in a residency where I was able to work with both surgeons and toenail clippers. It turned out that some doctors who clipped toenails were extremely talented surgeons. Alternatively, some high-volume surgeons had low-quality surgical results. Sitting on the floor to clip an eighty-year-old woman's toenails allowed the doctor time to chat and get to know her. They'd ask about how she enjoyed being a grandma, or who won her grandkids' T-ball games, and make special connections with them while providing them this service. *That* was something I wanted to experience with my patients.

And when I made a serious plan to follow in the footsteps of toenail clippers, I noticed something significant. They made the same income and often more than many of the big-shot surgeons.

This experience opened my eyes. What I learned was that sometimes doing the stuff that no one else wants to do puts you in a position to achieve more than anyone else will achieve. Finding that niche and then applying the grind worked for me as a pathway to making a mark on the world.

In the end, it doesn't matter what you do. Standing in the way of your success is whether or not you can do it well. As entrepreneur Malcolm Forbes said, "Diamonds are nothing more than chunks of coal that stuck to their jobs." It is the intense heat and pressure that forms one from the other.

You can be a podiatrist or a personal assistant. A painter or a plumber, like Earl Sears's friend. Earl Sears was a state congressman from Oklahoma who also happened to be the principal of Central Middle School, where most of my older siblings were educated. Everyone in the community—kids of executives to kids born on the wrong side of the tracks and everyone in between—adored him. He had an impeccable reputation for taking care of people.

And he always had time (and wanted) to sit down and talk with you. One of the things that he told me was the story of his friend. One day, his friend had told his father that he was going to take a job helping a plumber. His father was furious and told him it was a mistake. Plumbers, at the time, were not known for having high economic or social standing. He told him that he should spend the summer as an assistant at a law firm making less than helping this plumber. The "experience" of working at this firm would bode well on college applications and potentially get him into law school. He could hopefully one day come back as an associate attorney.

Following through on his desire to work for the plumber,

the friend became an apprentice. While in this role, he unclogged toilets and pipes, scrubbed the crud that gets wedged between the floor and the porcelain, and quickly learned the most efficient ways to brush the gunk out from the plumber's tools and from under his fingernails at the end of the day. In other words, he got really, really good at crappy work.

By the end of the summer, the plumber offered him a full-time job. He learned about installing pipes in new homes, building codes, and other ways plumbers can be useful. He advanced from an official apprentice to a journeyman and eventually a master plumber.

He became the plumber's business partner, taking some of the more physically demanding work that the retiring plumber couldn't do.

He became the sole owner once his mentor retired and expanded the business. From there he added multiple apprentices and journeymen. He grew that summer job into a small plumbing empire that led to more financial and social success than any "respectable" position his father could have ever hoped for. In the end, his dad saw the value in not what you do, but how you do it.

No matter what you do in life, if you do it well, you'll be successful. You could be cleaning toilets or clipping toenails. If you stick to the grind and sharpen yourself to be best, you'll have made it.

GET DIRTY, AND THEN GET READY TO PIVOT

Doing the dirty, unglamorous work will make you better, not worse. See the grind as an opportunity, not as a setback or something beneath you. When you apply yourself and work hard, you can utilize a challenge to launch yourself forward like drawing back a compound bow. Never forget: Two steps backward for three steps forward.

After my spinal fusion surgery, I had to do unglamorous work. There was no other choice. It wasn't hard, per se, but it was unglamorous physical therapy. It was necessary. Rather than being a setback, it taught me resilience, gratitude, and the importance of overcoming the challenges in front of me. To borrow Dolly Parton's phrase, if I wanted the rainbow, I had to put up with the rain.

The grind is an essential part of success in life in my experience. But just *because* you're grinding doesn't mean you're on the right trajectory. While you're working hard, it's extremely important to be open and able to change.

In other words, it's important to use the grind to your advantage. And if you aren't gaining an advantage—or if you end up facing a serious setback or unforeseen challenge—then you'll need to adapt. And pivoting is a choice you get to make, a conscious decision to change direction.

For example, in my experience as a partner of a corporate-structured company, I initially tried to stay quiet. I thought the right thing to do was to absorb what my veteran partners directed, stepping back and letting the experts handle things. I had to recognize this error and quickly adapt. My partner told me I needed to lean in more, not less. My input became highly valuable and critical to them, given that I was the only doctor in the partnership. I had to recognize my error and quickly correct the course. Our partnership immediately became better as I became more vocal and opinionated about the healthcare side of business.

You have to be a sailboat that harnesses the wind, that unseen natural force that is outside of our control. Sometimes it doesn't blow, sometimes it's gale-force, and sometimes it's not headed in the direction we want. But it's on us to catch it, take advantage of it, and turn it into a successful journey.

CHAPTER 3

THE PIVOT

"Success demands flexibility; those who pivot will prevail."

—UNKNOWN

Evolution shows that the most successful animal species are also the best at adapting.

My wife and I have experienced this firsthand since we began to raise animals on our property. We would call our animal situation a zoo, but it feels more like a circus. It's chaotic energy, as if there are clowns juggling on unicycles while acrobats fall into a net with a nearby ring on fire sitting just in front of the "tamed" lions. Our house is a spectacle.

But it's chaos created from the fact that we both grew up loving animals. My father had a handful of cows that he'd raise to either sell the meat or give it away as Christmas gifts. For him, it was a hobby. For my father-in-law, it was competitive. He was a buckle-winning rodeo cowboy who specialized in a flashy event called cowboy mounted hooting, where he'd ride on horseback through a course, firing his .44 revolvers at balloons.

We both grew up around livestock, but at first my wife only had a couple Chihuahuas. Then, one day, my wife said, "Hey, let's get the kids a pony for Christmas." The family ranch had space; it was 1,300 acres. She pressed, "Wouldn't it be fun to bring over our pony so the kids could go on long rides?" Yes, in fact, that did sound really fun. It sounded like a nice change.

My wife went with my father-in-law to some auctions to make it happen. Behind the scenes, I thought of a wonderfully romantic pivot. What if I bought my wife a horse? My father-in-law, with had more knowledge about horses than I did, helped me find the perfect one. Little did I know that she was doing the same thing for me. So that Christmas, the kids got a pony and both my wife and I received horses. The kids were over the moon. Anyone with kids knows that a pony is like the Taj Mahal of Christmas gifts for them. Then my in-laws joined in on the fun, and we went from zero horses to five very, very quickly.

Two horses and one pony in an average-sized backyard was pretty cramped. That didn't stop us from adding alpacas to the mix. We kept three in our backyard, named Cinnamon, Toast, and Crunch. From there, my wife really wanted to test the limits of the HOA. So she got a handful of chickens for eggs.

Shortly thereafter, we received notice that we had to get the animals out of the backyard. That's when we decided to move to a place that had more space—it ended up being two acres—where we could keep our animals.

Riding lessons started soon afterward for our kids. That evolved into participating in hunting, jumping, and equestrian-style competitions. We brought on a riding trainer, and that's when my wife pitched the idea of owning our own equestrian center. In July of 2021, that dream came true when she opened Timber Grove Equestrian Center, which currently houses about thirty horses and provides English-style riding lessons to more than fifty students between the ages of five and seventy-five!

End of story, right? Wrong. After being open for a while, we eventually added breeding horses to our list of services for clients. One result of that was a beautiful French Percheron named Neva that my wife gifted me for my fortieth birthday.

Close behind that, my wife decided that she wanted a miniature horse, which are just expensive lawn ornaments because you can't use them for anything. They're just there for looks. We traveled to several auctions in hopes of getting one, but it ended up not working out. So my wife pivoted. In the subsequent weeks, she sent me pictures of miniature Highland cows—perhaps the cutest animal on the face of the planet.

HOLY COW!

Going to auctions for Highland cows, though, took us a little bit out of our comfort zone, as far as the cost. We noticed that some of them could go for as high as $20,000. Steers were the most affordable, so we went ahead and got one. We named him TaTonka, the Lakota word for bison. And boy was he cute!

He was so cute that we kept watching those online Highland cow auctions. And we kept seeing baby heifers going for thousands of dollars. During one auction, my wife looked at me with an idea lighting up her eyes. "Maybe we could buy a heifer and make a little business out of this," she said. It was quite the change from our original intention. "Let's do it!" I replied.

Together, we created the Heavenly Cattle Company with the tagline, "The Original Holy Cow." We dove into the research to figure out how to breed the cutest miniature Highland cows.

We bought a couple more, including a bull to begin breeding. On a drive home one day, we stopped to bottle-feed the animals at those "pet relief areas" at gas stations. We knew we were on to something because, oh, the looks we would get. People started turning in to park, not getting gas but to pet our animals. Some were even making offers to buy them.

Today, our herd consists of ten cows and our bull, Norman, who became the mascot of our merchandise. Holy cow! Quite an adventure (or circus) has developed from the plan to buy our kids one pony.

But our pivoting through the years taught us a lot of important lessons. We learned how to run a variety of new businesses. We learned a lot about the new animals we were taking in. We learned a lot about ourselves, including the fact that we adapted well to taking on so many animals.

THE IMPORTANCE OF ADAPTATION

In the midst of everything we learned, perhaps the most important was the biggest difference between the horses, alpacas, and the Highland cows. Not all have the ability to adapt to their environment. Horses can be divas, sure. They need special grain to avoid digestive issues and their hooves are cleaned and shod regularly for them. A signal horse will get more dental work done than I will in my entire life. But they can at least adapt to their environment and put up a fight if cornered in nature by predators. On a safari trail ride in Kenya, we rode horses near a pride of three lions. We were so close we could even hear their loud breathing. Our guide, seeing the concern on our faces, assured us that lions do not bother horses. He shared stories of these lions attempting to approach the horses only for the horses' kicks and stomps to land several blows squarely on the lions. Apparently those lions now stayed clear from horses.

Similarly, cows use their horns, hooves, and tails to deter predators. A strong herd of cows can thwart off coyotes, wildcats, and even some bears. But unlike the delicate tummies of horses, cows have multichambered stomachs that help them eat a wider variety of things without digestive problems. And they're pretty resilient to diseases and infections. Our ranch has around one hundred cows that survive with very little human intervention. The cowboys come out to work them every few months, but they mostly just care for themselves. People always ask me, "You just leave the cows out there by themselves?" I chuckle and remind them that cows, horses, and other animals have survived without humans for thousands of years.

Alpacas are not the same as cows and horses. They are far less hearty. In fact, anything and everything kills them. They are, in a word, delicate. They get sick all the time. And the most dangerous thing for an alpaca is deer poop, as it contains a virus that attacks their nervous system. In the Piney Woods of southeast Texas, we have a bunch of deer, a bunch of deer poop, and not as many alpacas.

From a survivalist standpoint, alpacas have no real defense mechanisms. Sure, they can kick and spit a little bit, but they don't have any fight in them. And their hooves are soft-padded, so even if an anomalous alpaca had the courage and landed a kick, it would be like getting bopped with a pillow. It's far more likely that they'll just give up as soon as you grab them. This is not a fearsome species that we're talking about here.

Horses and cows, unlike alpacas, can pivot. They can adapt to the situation that they're in and fight for survival. Alpacas? Not so much. Unfortunately, we don't have alpacas on our property anymore. It's too difficult to keep them alive. But as Charles Darwin wrote, "It is not the strongest of the species that survive, nor the most intelligent, but the one most responsive to change." The same is true for humans as much as it is for animals.

PICK YOURSELF OUT OF THE MUCK

Similarly to horses and cows—animals that can pivot and adapt—my wife and I decided to continually adapt and evolve after we bought our kids their first pony. One new thing led to another. Notice, then, that adapting is not just a story of surviving and thriving (success) but also one of joy. If it weren't for that first pivot—my wife and I gifting each other a horse to complement our kids' pony—none of the subsequent animal adventures and the joys they've given us would have been possible.

In my professional life, the same thing is true. The ability to pivot has been a secret ingredient to success. When it comes to your situation, being open to adaptation could be a crucial approach on your path to success.

What exactly does the pivot provide? In our unique journeys, things don't always go as planned, intended, or desired. These are called happy accidents—opportunities to learn—and they require that you evolve. If we can't learn and adjust, we won't progress. We won't grow. We won't be on a successful trajectory. How do I know? One of the moments of clarity about the pivot came in my unique journey while playing high school football.

One of my high school football coaches, Coach Gene Stahlman, happened to be a former drill sergeant in the military. It was clear that he'd transferred his skills in the armed forces to his role in sports. Me and the other players may have been wearing football uniforms, but he yelled at us as if we were wearing military uniforms. He wasn't mean or nasty. But he was intense, breaking you down to build you up.

Getting yelled at is one thing, but I should also mention it was accompanied by the most noxious practice environment. Our high school expanded its footprint over the years and was eventually built out. The football field ended up right next door to a sewage treatment facility. There was no escaping that smell. During practice, the combination of stench and screaming really made it feel like a boot camp.

Back then, football practices had drinking water constantly streaming out of PVC pipes for hydration. But it made the field muddy and gross. Coach Stahlman would have us do drills in this muck. You'd finish just covered in filth—stinky, sticky, and hot.

Without fail, during a drill on this muddy field, a player would mess up, look up sheepishly, and offer some excuse as to why they did it wrong. That excuse was a fatal mistake. Even if it was valid, Coach Stahlman, with his military crew cut and pale, Viking-like visage turning redder, would reply with his motto: "Improvise! Adapt! Overcome!" I found out later that this was the unofficial slogan of the US Marines. When we heard that phrase, we'd put our heads down, try harder, and usually become the best version of ourselves.

Improvise, adapt, and overcome. Since my days playing for Coach Stahlman, those words have always stuck with me. They helped me learn that your circumstances don't really matter. It doesn't matter if somebody else is to blame. It doesn't matter if things are stacked against you. You need to improvise. You need to adapt. And you need to overcome.

To me, all of those things are part of *the pivot*—or making the necessary adjustments to make something work.

POWERBOATS AND SAILBOATS

That wasn't the only experience I had in education that taught me to pivot. Another experience came years later while attending Brigham Young University. My first organic chemistry class in college was typical for large universities. The lectures were held in a large auditorium with more than three hundred students.

When it came time to work in smaller groups, it was in a laboratory setting with one teacher's assistant per every dozen or so students. My specific TA was Japanese and didn't speak very much English. And the "professor's assistant" (PA, usually a grad student) was from Uganda and also spoke very little English. Organic chemistry is already a difficult course that cuts the "wheat from the chaff." I couldn't understand some concepts even when explained in perfect English! I made an appointment to meet with the professor to see what I could do to improve my grades.

When I walked in to the appointment, he didn't lift his eyes from whatever he was reading and writing. He simply said, "How can I help you?" It was in a bored voice that probably asked that same question twenty times a day to students just like me. I needed to talk to him, so that didn't deter me. I explained that I was trying to get my grades up but wasn't sure what my options were. Still staring down, he asked, "Are you a powerboat or a sailboat?"

"Uh, I don't know," was my confused reply.

He continued, "You need to be a powerboat." That was it. That's all he said. I stood there, waiting for a follow-up or additional details of how powerboats related to my dilemma. That follow-up never came.

I thought it over. He was trying to tell me that I needed to be more ambitious, more aggressive, and power myself through any wind or wave. It was good, insightful advice, and it reminded me of Coach Stahlman. Use your fuel to overcome.

But there's hardly a day that goes by where I don't think about powerboats and sailboats and their true differences. Powerboats use fuel combustion, an engine, and a propeller to push themselves through the water. Big waves, small waves, it doesn't matter. The powerboat will get you there.

On the other hand, sailboats can't churn the water without fuel and machinery. A sailboat harnesses the unseen power of the wind and adapts to its circumstances to get where it's going. It might not get there in a straight line, but it gets there. It improvises, adapts, and overcomes. It manipulates the elements of the environment to move toward a desired destination.

I don't know if I'm a powerboat or a sailboat. I'd like to think I'm more of a sailboat. Powerboats seem more like a type A personality—that strong, ambitious, cutthroat mindset. Most people aren't built like that. For everyone else, in order to succeed and thrive, we have to make the most of our environment—to harness the wind in order to maintain a path toward success.

By embracing the pivot and adjusting to what life has thrown my way, I have defined my personal and professional journey and put myself directly on the path toward success. And I have no doubt that it can work for you, too. But I want to offer you very distinct moments in my career where I *had* to pivot.

I offer them chronologically. With any of them, you may find yourself at a similar crossroads. My hope is that they help you realize that you're not alone in facing the need to adjust to your circumstances. You, too, can make adjustments to maintain a successful trajectory. You, too, can improvise, adapt, and overcome.

PIVOT 1: MY AMAZING SISTER

I'm the seventh of eight kids. The eighth kid is my sister, Katie. When she was born, the doctors didn't think she'd survive more than a few weeks. A few weeks came and went. Then they said a few months. Then a few years. By the time she was eight years old, they had finally come up with a diagnosis; she had Prader–Willi syndrome.

This syndrome is defined by the brain's inability to feel full from food. Anybody with it could eat a triple-decker cheeseburger then top it off with an entire extra-large pizza. The moment they took the last bite of that pizza, it would feel like they hadn't eaten for a week.

We've all felt a little bit hungry, but I doubt anybody reading this has ever truly been starving. My little sister, Katie, from the day she was born and throughout the forty years of her life, has never felt anything except starvation. That is the burden of Prader–Willi syndrome.

In addition to that difficult truth, we also understood that she could end up eating herself to death since she never felt full. Prader–Willi syndrome is not common, and our family had to adapt to support her.

We were given instructions by the doctors. We had to control our home in such a way that kept Katie alive. So, unlike normal households, we had to use a chain and padlock to keep the fridge closed. The pantry and cabinets all had locks and keys. It would be frustrating when a key would get lost and I couldn't get to some Pop-Tarts after school, but this was necessary for our family.

Katie was smart! We had to hide those keys so that Katie couldn't find them. Sometimes she'd find them, and we'd have to find a new hiding spot. Because of that experience, I bet you that my sister Amy and I are abnormally good at finding places to hide keys in a standard kitchen. If food was left out, Katie would find it, eat it, or hide it for later. If left to herself, she would slowly kill herself with food.

Once she understood that finding a key or learning a code meant we'd put it in a new hiding spot or buy a new padlock, she learned how to be sneaky by putting the key back after she ate. She learned not to mess up the pantry too much. She knew if we placed a bag of chips with the label facing outward and folded twice, she would need to put it back in that exact same way or else she would be caught. She would also hide food. I can recall an incident in front of friends, digging my hand into the couch cushions looking for the TV remote only to come up with a half-eaten stick of butter and a chunk of rotisserie chicken.

Prader–Willi syndrome also comes with some cognitive development issues. Katie hasn't grown up on the same trajectory as most people. When she was twelve, she acted like she was three. When she was twenty, she acted like she was twelve. She's never really developed much beyond that. But she's still sharp as a tack.

That sharpness intensifies when she goes into survival mode. When someone feels like they are starving, they will go to any length to eat. We've all seen those survival films where people are stranded without food. Earthworms or maggots start to look appealing after days without food. If hungry enough, people will literally kill each other for food. Katie was no exception.

It wasn't unusual for Katie to pull a knife, throw pictures from off the walls, and make hollow threats. In an attempt to feed her satiated-but-cognitively-hungry body, Katie would do what anyone starving would do to survive. I remember my sweet, saintly mom telling Katie that she wasn't allowed to do something because she had snuck some food. In that instance, weighing in at over three hundred pounds, Katie went primal and attempted to smother our mom.

Now, my mom is a tough lady. She raised her two little brothers into all-American wrestlers and could roughhouse with her five wild boys. But, small-framed and barely taller than five feet, she couldn't keep Katie from pushing her to the ground and lying on top of her. Our grandmother happened to be living with us at that time and, being even smaller and much older than my mom. During the struggle, my mom was fighting for air and telling Katie she couldn't breath. Katie replied by saying she was going to kill her. (Remember, my little sister doesn't have much understanding of right versus wrong). My little grandma quickly grabbed a phone and dialed 911.

You can imagine the heartache incidents like this caused, knowing that this poor girl was starving and willing to do whatever it took because she was so hungry. And when you're faced with that kind of drive from somebody willing to do whatever it takes, it takes quite a bit of discipline to continue pivoting. We had to be steadfast and not give her what she wanted because she'd most likely die otherwise.

Circumstances changed around Katie moment by moment. And the stakes to constantly make the necessary adjustments couldn't be greater. We were fighting for her life. Over time, the changes we made put us onto a path that ended up being the most successful—as learning and reiterating often lead to success.

There's about a forty-five-minute period after she's eaten where she can acknowledge that she just ate. We'd say something like, "I know that you're hungry, but you just ate. Can you wait forty-five minutes until you can eat something else?"

From this, we all developed a system where she would eat small amounts of food every forty-five minutes throughout the day.

The best part was that it normalized Katie. It seemed to be the first time that we could rationalize with her around food. She would be agreeable knowing that she could eat food again in a short time. An episode of *Unsolved Mysteries* would consume most of that time.

But after the smothering incident with my mom, everything changed. After the police were called and my mom was rescued, the State of Oklahoma intervened. They recognized that Katie nor the family was entirely safe. So the difficult and heartbreaking decision was made to put Katie into twenty-four-hour supervised care, which started at the Ronald McDonald House in Kansas City. I will forever be grateful for that charity. They helped her (and us) figure out the best ways to treat her Prader-Willi syndrome. Doctors spent weeks with Katie and other special-needs children where little medical research was available. My mom spent weeks off and on with Katie for the next two years.

To a lesser degree than my sister, her moving out required me to pivot again. I didn't have the junior and senior year of high school that my friends had. I didn't get to give my mom flowers on Senior Day. She was in Arizona, St. Louis, or Kansas City with my sister.

During those important, formative years, I had to adjust to my circumstances and learn how to take care of myself. She did continue to take care of me from afar; don't get me wrong. I am forever grateful to have had her in my life at that time. But there are certain things that a mother brings to a son that cannot be replicated when she's not around. I'm not sad or bitter; I'm a better person because of it. It was an early lesson.

Later, my family supplicated a friend, State Congressman

Ernest Istook, for some sort of help. Soon after, Mr. Istook passed legislation in Oklahoma that allowed Prader–Willi and other special-needs children to be housed together in state-funded, twenty-four-hour care. This groundbreaking resource saw Prader–Willi youth from all over the country find a healthy, safe, and friendly home. The best part was that Katie could once again be close to her family. She has spent the last twenty-five years in Tulsa with amazing caregivers and my family.

Because the entire family embraced the need to improvise and overcome, we helped Katie overcome. Adaptation is a profound process. It's part and parcel not only to survival but to success. It forced our whole family, my sister included, to learn unique lessons in patience, caring, tolerance, and, above all, pivoting.

PIVOT 2: PREDENTAL TO PODIATRY

Sometimes in life we are faced with a life-changing choice.

When I started studying at Brigham Young University, I had planned on becoming a dentist like my father. My oldest brother-in-law was also a dentist who, back in Oklahoma, had three growing clinics that were very successful. At first, it looked like I was on the right path to graduate and join one of those clinics to contribute to its growth.

But when it came time, I noticed that *a lot* of people were pursuing dentistry. BYU, where I studied, produces around 290 annual graduates that go on to dental school. And this was just one university. I quickly realized that dentistry could become a saturated market in some areas. When I started to look around and pay attention to how many dentists I could see while driving around, there were dental clinics on just about every corner of town.

In spite of this, I had a plan and I was going to stick to it. So I applied to a few dental schools. Dental school application was a tedious process. I can't imagine it's become any better now. They might as well have just asked you for your kidney.

And if you happened to get invited to visit a campus, it was another huge ordeal. At one on-campus visit, I was greeted, hosted, interviewed, and dismissed by current first-year students. I didn't talk to faculty, staff, upperclassmen, or a dean of admissions. On a second visit, I was able to briefly talk with a faculty member, who just told me how great their dental school was.

Because dental school application, interview, and acceptance processes were so difficult, I began to fear I wouldn't make it. It dawned on me that becoming a dentist might not be in the cards for me.

A friend of mine, Doug, was in a similar situation. He was predental like me and faced the realities of a saturated dental market back home and highly competitive, overflowing dental schools. One day Doug asked, "Have you ever thought about podiatry school?" I told him, "I don't know if I want to work exclusively with children," confusing podiatry with pediatrics. "No," he said, "it's a foot doctor."

He continued by explaining to me the huge demand for podiatrists, both at that time and the expected demand into the future. And the nine podiatry schools across the country, he mentioned, were taking anybody with a pulse.

I didn't have a ton of options. And I wasn't so much in love with people's dirty mouths that I couldn't pivot to dirty feet. So I gave it a chance. When you are thrown curveballs, you have to adjust your swing to hit the ball. It was the same improvisation that I experienced trying to help my sister.

To start, I applied to three podiatry schools, having just

learned about podiatry in April with classes starting in June. It was a process of adapting, improvising, and overcoming. One school was in New York, one was in Ohio, and the other was in Chicago.

Dental and podiatry schools' interview processes are very different. The first school I cold-called put me on directly with the dean of admissions. They actually went out of their way to set up a meeting with me.

I went to New York first. There weren't any expectations, but I had spent a lot of time in some rough parts of Mexico City for two years, so I figured that nothing I ran into in New York would surprise me. The day of the interview, I stepped out of the subway and saw a man urinating on the wall making no effort to hide what he was doing. It was a bit of a reality check.

I was wearing a khaki suit with a pastel necktie, trying my best to look like Matthew McConaughey in *A Time to Kill*. It would be more accurate, though, to say I looked like a circus clown at a formal wedding. Looking around, it occurred to me that I stuck out a little bit.

Looking to burn time since I was nervous and early, I decided to grab a McDonald's breakfast before my interview. I stepped through the door to the Golden Arches. It felt like that moment in a Western film where the guy walks into the saloon and everybody stops what they're doing to look at him. But instead of stunned silence, there was noise and chaotic energy all around me. An employee and a customer were screaming at each other with fists clenching balls of fabric from each other's shirts. Nobody cared to intervene or even noticed it at all. People in line were too busy yelling about how slow the lines were moving. Staff were still taking orders at the other registers and customers were paying attention to their McGriddle and coffee. A manager came from the kitchen area, walked right past the altercation and started yelling at a homeless man who was walking around eating off other people's tables. Two cops were by the bathroom putting someone in handcuffs, and an old woman was elbow deep in one of the trash cans. It was madness. And it was eight in the morning.

The interview itself was fantastic, but I knew that I wouldn't be able to survive in New York. I felt like a worm in that Big Apple. I had plans to propose to my future wife, and that atmosphere was just a little too aggressive for me to feel comfortable starting a family. You have to be tough to live in New York.

It was different in Cleveland. I felt more at ease and invited. When I walked into the dean's office in Ohio, she was kind, warm, and genuinely interested in my story. She said, "We'd love for you to be part of our program." Then she asked me about the last book I had read. Being a history nerd for World War II, it happened to be *World at War* by Gerhard L. Weinberg. Almost like a fortune teller, she replied, "You read a book like that because you're a natural leader, and our school needs and wants somebody like you." It felt like the school actually wanted me. That I wouldn't just be a number. It also helped that they had just installed a multimillion-dollar anatomy lab and were in the process of building a forty-acre campus.

I left there feeling like this was meant to be, so I never visited Chicago and enrolled in the Ohio College of Podiatric Medicine. It was one of the best pivots of my life. Without it, you wouldn't be reading these words today.

PIVOT 3: HEALTHY PATIENTS, HEALTHY BUSINESSES

The major difference between med school and podiatry school is that *everything* in podiatry school is geared toward the foot.

Many different systems are covered—musculoskeletal, vascular, nerve, and dermatology—but everything is about the foot. Of course, the various systems of the body *are* taught. We learn about the heart, lungs, brain, nervous system, and everything else. But we learn about them in the context of treating problems in the lower extremities.

This means that we are very hyperfocused from day one on diseases and problems with the foot. By the second year, I was going on rotations with our professors and staff podiatrists as part of our education. We shadowed them in clinic, surgeries, and hospitals and spent hours in their lectures on campus. The school was good at bringing in podiatrists of all types for the different rotations. We learned the anatomy of the foot, the biomechanics of how the foot worked while walking, skin disorders associated with the foot, and systemic diseases involving the foot. We spent every day for four years learning about the foot.

By the end of my third year, I got to meet one Dr. Berkowitz, who had already been practicing for decades. He worked with his son, and together they were a great duo to learn from. He did things a bit old school, using X-ray film processing, using paper billing and paper charting. I don't think there was a single computer in the office.

I recall we were about to go in and see a patient, and he showed me his handwritten notes on her chart to help me prep, too. Most practitioners have a lengthy chart overflowing with patient information like their insurance, personal information, long lists of medicines, previous surgeries, family history, and detailed specifics of their previous encounters with the doctor. All he had written down were short details about her and her family. A little blurb saying that her grandson started playing T-ball. One note read, "Granddaughter is getting married this summer in Mexico." He included little bits of clinical documentation, like what was bothering her and what he recommended her treatment should be, but they were accompanied by personal details not involving her feet. His notes were humanizing—things that let his patients know that he, the doctor, cared about them. The more I studied his notes, the more personal stories I saw. One read, "Lost her husband a week ago, funeral on Friday, send flowers." Another read, "Feet hurt from grandson's baseball tournament, but they won!"

That was the first lesson I received in what we call *patient management*. The doctor-to-patient connection was important. Good bedside manners would give patients confidence in your care. A nervous patient suffering from "white-coat anxiety" (doctors traditionally wear white lab coats) could find comfort in doctors who simply care.

Dr. Berkowitz was a very, very good doctor of podiatric medicine. But he was also great at the business of podiatric medicine. He had a passion that went beyond just the treatment of patients. It was a passion for his patients but also to cultivate his business. That idea—to grow a business and make business choices as a self-employed doctor—were not topics that were covered at school.

He helped me pivot my thinking and prepare for the future. No longer was I thinking only about how to be a great podiatrist; now I was thinking about how to be a great podiatrist *and* run a great clinic.

As time went on, Dr. Berkowitz caught me up to speed in short order. He had three top priorities…three pearls of wisdom. Patients first. He argued that a strong clinic will implement the treatments that, above all else, help the patients. Second, those treatments need to be covered by insurance to reduce out-of-pocket costs less or be worth whatever costs the patients would spend. And third, a good clinic does the things that are actually good for the business (i.e., make money).

Generally speaking, healthcare professionals try to avoid associating treatment with business and money. But we really can't; they're tied together. You can't provide the best care to your patients when you go out of business.

Learning this gave me confidence in opening up my own clinic right out of residency. And now, this pivot is clearly the basis for my current work with Allevio, helping clinics across the country adjust their business practices in order to better serve their patients (most importantly) and also their bottom line.

PIVOT 4: THE RESIDENCY SCRAMBLE

Near the end of podiatry school, there is a scheduled day where students get matched with a residency program to continue their studies. It's called Match Day.

There is so much anticipation for Match Day, it feels a little bit like Christmas morning, running to the tree to see what Santa brought. But it also comes with a healthy dose of dread. Hopefully it wouldn't be coal under that tree.

All of this stress and excitement is created by the somewhat smoke-and-mirrors approach to the whole thing. Students rank their top four choices. Residency programs rank their top four students. If you ranked a program number one and they ranked you number one, then boom! That was a match. But the program didn't always have direct matches like that, so the algorithm would put the next-best matches together until all of the available residency positions were filled. If programs A and B both ranked a student number one, the student would be matched with whichever they chose higher. If the student ranked program C higher than A and B, the student would match with C and the other programs would move to their second choice.

But of course things were even more complicated than that. The year I graduated, there was a shortage of residency positions available to all of the graduating students nationwide. It was projected that around twenty-five students would graduate and not have a residency program available. This problem hadn't been properly anticipated between podiatry schools and residency programs, essentially meaning that these graduating student-doctors had to wait a year. They'd have to reinterview and apply with the following year's graduating class.

It was a bit like if *Game of Thrones* mixed with *Hunger Games*. There was a lot of secrecy. Nobody would share which residency programs they were choosing, and the residency programs only revealed their first choice. There was a lot of deception and maneuvering by students to get the programs they wanted and vice versa.

Because my wife was from Houston, I ranked two programs there. My first choice was a program in rural Ohio near our home, having liked the community I had gotten to know over the years in school. My wife had an incredible job in Ohio, and we bought our first home there.

I got along great with the chief resident and program director, so I anticipated they'd want me, too. The Ohio program told me throughout my rotations that I would be considered. By the end of my externship, it seemed all but certain. Right before Match Day, I was confident that if I wanted a spot with them, it was mine. That program only had one spot every year but I felt confident and assured that I was their choice. The Texas programs started to feel like backup plans.

It turned out that Ohio didn't pick me as their first choice. I was second. They went with their first choice. I didn't rank high enough with the highly-sought-after programs in Houston, so Match Day started with me getting a lump of coal. Without a match for a residency program, I started to panic. I was dejected and immediately concerned about my professional future. I didn't have much of a choice but to put my head down and grind. For those in my position, we had to improvise, adapt, and overcome—a process we termed "the scramble."

The scramble is the immediate calamity that nonmatched students and unfilled residency programs go through after the program matches are released. Each side experiences their own form of chaos.

Programs with multiple available positions might have only filled three and, wanting to get the best resident still available, start dialing available candidates. Residency programs have all of their residents, new and old, join in on the soliciting process.

Students who didn't match can, with the help of their school, see which residency programs still have availability and who to contact for the position. Those of us scrambling start calling every residency program with a listed phone number to see if any of them might have an unexpected opening.

In total, it's chaos. Both sides are scrambling to secure residents and residencies that are best for all parties, no students wanting to become part of the group of twenty-five that gets left behind.

So I scrambled. Some students would make or receive one call and all the pressure and worry would dissolve. I remember one frustrated student throwing up his hands and quitting before attempting to scramble. He didn't even attempt to land a spot. He ended up graduating as a doctor of podiatric medicine and took a job at a sporting goods store. Whatever you do, do it well.

It was terrifying. I imagine it's like NFL Draft prospects who expect to get picked in the first round, only to fall down the draft board. The camera is on them. They're getting fidgety. Maybe their agent calls them to calm them down a little bit. But they're getting really nervous that they won't get drafted. It's panic-inducing.

During this process, I was calling every program with availability. It didn't matter where or how sought after the program. I called, sent my résumé, and put myself out there. While taking a breath between frantic phone calls, I received a call from a residency director whom I rotated with out of Houston. His program was my second choice and they were taking three residents that year but had only filled two positions. He immediately offered a position to me, recalling that I used to bring the other residents bagels each week. I was only there for six weeks, but the bagels made me memorable. (Sometimes it pays to bring people food. Read more about the power of differentiation in Chapter 5.)

He offered me a position. I had been saved! Even better, I'd end up in Houston, which was the city of my top choices. Within a few days, I went from not having anywhere to go to taking my wife and infant son back to Texas.

It took a pivot—the scramble—to land a residency position. I wouldn't accept the results from Match Day and just delay my life a year, thus my openness to adapt to my circumstances helped me find success.

PIVOT 5: SURGERIES, ACCOLADES, AND TOENAILS, OH MY!

I did my residency at the Kingwood Medical Center in Houston, Texas. The first year for any profession is always the grunt year. You're used and abused. It's long hours, long days, and long weeks. For me, it wasn't uncommon to sleep at the hospital since I was on call. For any residents reading this currently working at Kingwood Medical Center, I highly advise the beds in the maternity ward. They're the most comfortable, and it's not even close.

Whenever my on-call pager buzzed, it was one of two things. I would get pulled into a surgery and have to stand like a statue for three hours retracting who-knows-what body part or organ. Or, I was pulled into the emergency room to sew up a wound or laceration that the nurses didn't want to bother with. It turned out the podiatry residents at Kingwood were renowned to be the best at sutures. Even more than podiatry school, residency emphasized and focused on surgery, especially of complicated pathology with complex surgical treatments.

Then there were the case conferences, clinical reports, presentations, journal discussions, and a huge emphasis on didactic education. And since it was all happening in a short period of time, you had to do your best to absorb everything.

Once in a blue moon, you would assist in a podiatry surgery as a first-year resident. And that was something to look forward to. It was even more exciting to get something complicated, like Achilles tendon repairs or ankle fusions. Within that environment, many residents get swept into thinking that success as physicians was in doing large, complicated surgeries; being published in journals; being invited to lecture at conferences; and so on.

It wasn't the case when I shadowed actual podiatry private

practices. I noticed that more than half of their business was clipping toenails. School had taught us that we would treat toenail problems. Yet, nobody in residency actually talked about clipping toenails, shaving calluses, removing ingrown nails, or other "simpler" parts of our profession. When they did, it would be dismissive like, "Oh, this next patient is *just* toenails," as if that patient encounter would teach me as much as mulling over X-rays of an ankle fracture.

Because of this professional neurosis, podiatrists like to find ways to puff out our chests and say, "You see! I *am* a real doctor!" I was guilty of that, too. My desire to perform the most complicated surgeries led to me being one of the first residents to graduate with a Reconstructive Rearfoot/Ankle Accreditation from the program. That was fancy talk for doing a lot of successful major surgeries. We kept these kinds of accolades like currency. All I needed was to flash it, and it meant that I was a "better" doctor.

Everything was surgery. There was no education about the small and valuable things like bedside manner, practice management, clipping toenails, shaving calluses, and other bread-and-butter components to podiatry.

There was even a hierarchical ranking system. The third-years got to pick the surgeries they wanted, and the first-years were left to fend over the scraps. And that kind of educational environment shapes the larger professional environment. It's no wonder then that, when residents graduate, they continue to pursue surgeries and accolades first and foremost. There's a saying that if all you have is a hammer, everything you see is a nail.

The bottom line is this: Didactics and basic treatment is something that's necessary but not fun. On the other hand, surgery is something that's fun but not always necessary. So, that tends to influence young doctors in pursuing a career in complex surgeries. It's more fun (and gives you more accolades).

Now, I will say that the big-time doctors fighting for the complex surgeries were awesome, amazing people. I'm truly blessed to have been able to work with some of the best doctors in Houston. I learned so much from them.

And I also learned from doctors outside of the residency program. On days we weren't scheduled for surgery, we were allowed to visit affiliated practices. I'd go into the clinic and shadow a podiatrist as they met with patients. That, to me, was always more valuable than sitting in an operating room. I liked to see how the front desk person, the medical assistants, and all these other people interacted with the patients. I liked to watch different methods on how to shoot the breeze with patients to help them feel at ease.

The doctors I shadowed were aware of the biases that favored complex surgery. They'd warn me if a patient only required getting their toenails clipped, as if it wouldn't provide anything valuable to me or were themselves ashamed of clipping toenails for a living. It surprised me. I knew that if I wanted to find success, I would have to buck the trend.

It made me think, *Who is the best at clipping toenails in the world? They would have to be a successful person.* And that question kept passing through my mind. The management of toenails didn't pay a whole lot, but every patient needed that treatment. And they were always so grateful to have their toenails clipped rather than a more invasive form of treatment. The surgery patients, on the other hand, always seemed to be unhappy with the results. They always felt like they should be recovering slightly faster than they were.

That's when I started to think, *I need to pivot away from the big stuff and focus on the small stuff.* I didn't ignore the big stuff. I knew it would be important to excel in those areas when they came up, but the truth of the matter was that most days I would be seeing patients with toenail issues. Complex ankle fractures aren't happening daily.

Because clipping and caring for ailing toenails is an ongoing issue that countless patients face, adapting to the bread and butter would ensure that I was always working, that I was always in demand. So I gave up the glamorous life of a surgeon. For me, it was toenails or bust. That gave me the space to think more about practice management, which acted as the foundation of my future success.

It would be a while before I had my own practice, but that didn't mean I couldn't study up on how to run one successfully.

PIVOT 6: ALL RIVERS FLOW TO THE OCEAN

Opening up my own practice was intimidating. It didn't help that most of the people at my residency program dismissed me as naive or blind to the reality of running a business. Where I could, my goal was to mitigate the influence of these negative forces. It turns out wisdom doesn't come with a birthday cake. It comes with a never-ending cycle of experience. And you can only have an experience if you dive in and are willing to move with the current along the way.

The first question to answer when opening my practice was location. Where did I want to be? And if you are looking to run your own business, I think it is the most important question. Whenever I get students, residents, or doctors coming to me and looking for advice on opening their own practice, that's my opening question. "*Where* do you want to practice?"

First, you pick where you want to go, then make it work.

Too often people do the reverse. They'll go to the opportunity but then hate where they are. Maybe they aren't close to family, in a temperate or geographical area that's not pleasing to them, or a state that has high taxes…or something. Then they waste three years of their life before they realize they want to practice somewhere they want to live.

One way my practice could succeed, I thought, was to go to an area that was underserved. If the demand for a podiatrist surpassed the supply, I'd automatically be competitive in that area, right? But while building a business where there was little competition would be easier on the front end, it would probably cap how big I could grow it.

My wife and I knew that we wanted to be in the Houston area, specifically the north side. The best area on the north side of Houston is a place called the Woodlands. It's a master-planned community that is perennially named one of the best places to live in America. In the eighties, when construction began, it was the largest master-planned community in the country. With an unbelievable economy, it has been home to many global companies, PGA-level golf courses, and beautiful wooded scenery.

You can bet that this area attracted a lot of doctors. Many of Houston's top physicians lived in the Woodlands. And because they didn't want to drive all the way into Houston's world-class medical center, a miniature medical center and hospital eventually developed, which offers many of the same medical services provided in Houston. And the Woodlands is right next to I-45, connecting Houston to Dallas, ensuring a steady flow of patients.

So, I had a choice to make. Did I want to open a practice right next to a great hospital and close to a major freeway in the midst of great competition? Or, did I want to go to a more rural area, where there would be an easier startup by fulfilling an underserved area needing more podiatry? I asked my father-in-law his opinion and, like he always has, he gave me sage advice. My father-in-law was born and raised in Houston, went to the University of Houston, and started and retired his career in Houston. As a true Houstonian and successful businessman, I figured he would have valuable insight.

He started talking to me about water. "All streams become creeks that flow into rivers, and all rivers flow to the ocean," he began. Then he explained how all big cities in the world historically started near bodies of water, in part due to the accessibility to trade resources.

He continued, "Interstate 45 is like the Mississippi River. Thousands upon thousands of people drive up and down every day to work." He explained that economies thrive where there are people and prosperity. This is usually closer to larger population masses. The Woodlands grew in large part because of how easily accessible it was for wealthy Texas oilmen looking to leave the big city. He added, "People travel from all over to do things in the Woodlands. If they aren't seeing their doctor, they are shopping, attending events, or enjoying barbecure, Tex-Mex, or a steak house. If you set up in the Woodlands, you won't have a hard time growing, you'll just have to be better than your competition." Following that advice, I put my practice in the Woodlands, where there would be the most traffic.

The trade-off was that the Woodlands was also highly competitive. It was a clear pivot from my original thinking. And how did it turn out? There is no way I would have had as much career success had I gone anywhere else. Yes, it was more competitive. But that forced me to adjust to those circumstances and work harder to become a better doctor. Iron sharpens iron, as they say. And that was true for me. Understanding how traffic and flow of people would help me build my practice all came from learning about how all water flows to the ocean.

BE FLEXIBLE, BE A CHAMELEON

During residency, one of my coresidents called me a chameleon. I didn't know if it was a compliment or an insult, so I asked her to explain what that meant. She continued, "You seem to adapt to whatever group or person you're with." She told me that I would adjust how I spoke, my topics of conversation, and overall temperament to match the colleague, patient, or doctor I was speaking with. That made sense to me; I sincerely like finding things in common with people. I think everyone does. I wasn't intentionally changing my accent or personality based on the people or topic, but I was reading the room and adjusting to be more of myself (for good or bad). I was trying to empathize and better understand our conversations.

Something that has worked for me in finding success is the ability to adapt to my environment and circumstances. Be flexible, or as entrepreneur Cheryl Amyx says, "Don't panic. Pivot." That flexibility—the ability to pivot without skipping a beat—keeps the dance of life going. With it, you are always one step away from the next success, however big or small.

Are you flexible enough? Or are you too rigid in your mindset? Push yourself toward your dream destination by utilizing and adjusting to your environment and circumstances. You might view your circumstances in a negative light. But, to me, they're not. They are just the circumstances. Springboard off of them. Harness them like a sailboat harnesses wind.

If you are able to do that—to be flexible—you can face most any challenge. No matter what happens, if you put in the effort and action, then you'll get the reward and consequences you're after.

PART 2

BUILDING YOUR UNIQUE PATH TO SUCCESS

CHAPTER 4

THE REWARD OF EFFORT

"A dream doesn't become reality through magic; it takes sweat, determination, and hard work."

—COLIN POWELL

Whether you're in the middle of the grind, a pivot, or both, it's going to take hard work to succeed.

A grandson of Polish immigrants, my dad learned about hard work very young.

His grandparents arrived in Oklahoma via Chicago after arriving at Ellis Island. My father became the last of his name the moment his grandparents arrived at the terminal. Josef Walenty Waclaw (pronounced vah-LEN-tee VAH-clav), changed his name at Ellis Island to Joseph Valentine Vaclaw. Vaclaw was/is a common Slovakian given name but rarely ever found as a surname. Although we don't know for sure, it was likely at Ellis Island that the immigration official transcribing the name misheard it and wrote Vaclaw. It was after a short stop in Chicago that they moved to the oil capital of the west, Oklahoma.

Many immigrants, including the Polish, were known to be very, very hard workers. But like so many other immigrants, they didn't have much when they arrived. And when they did arrive in the 1930s, the US economy was going through the Great Depression. If that weren't bad enough, Oklahoma was in the midst of the dust bowl. It was just devastating to be in that part of the country. They settled in Bartlesville, the hometown of Frank Phillips (founder of Phillips 66). It was a small, oil-boom town a few miles from the northern border with Kansas. Being the strong-natured immigrants that they were, they took a job that few other people wanted, working for oil companies.

Although they were not rich in finances, these first Vaclaws were rich in family. My father had two aunts with no kids of their own, so they spent their time doting on him. As an only child with virtually three sets of parents, he was wealthy in nonmaterial things. But they were poverty stricken, like most Oklahomans were coming out of the dust bowl era.

Because of this mixture of oil tycoons and laborers, Bartlesville was a strange mix of the very, very wealthy and people from humble circumstances. That created a very unique environment for a childhood upbringing, in that my dad became very aware that he grew up on the wrong side of the tracks.

He lived in a very small, humble house. He'd tell me stories about how he'd see wealthy oilmen all over town. "Boots Adams," he once recalled, "was a pipeline man who would drive past our school every day in his Cadillac." Standing outside one hot summer day, Mr. Adams let my dad and his friends feel the air-conditioning through a window. It was the first car in town that had air-conditioning.

Sometimes the neighborhood kids would run up next to it, like they were following an ice-cream truck or something. But these kids didn't want ice cream or air-conditioning. They were just in awe. When the car stopped, Boots and his wife, Barbara, would step out dressed in fancy clothes and freshly shined shoes.

That Cadillac was itself like a local celebrity. And anytime it rolled through town, my dad would tell his friends, "One day, I'm going to own a Cadillac like that." My dad always mentioned that specific story when recalling his childhood. He knew what he wanted and had Polish determination to get it. One day during my own childhood, he came home with a peach-colored Cadillac DeVille. Despite being born into poverty, my dad had a vision of where he wanted to get in life. He wanted to take the strong family connection that he had and add financial stability. He didn't want to scrape by, but he didn't want to be extremely wealthy. He just wanted to provide his family with certain comforts...and drive a Cadillac.

That motivation helped my dad turn toward a life of effort and action to achieve the rewards and consequences he wanted. Throughout his entire life up until he stopped driving, my dad always leased a Cadillac. The very first one he brought home was a two-door DeVille. Mind you, he had eight children. Somehow Mom allowed him to drive a two-door car.

A PLUS *B* EQUALS *C*

His childhood was such that it earned him a lifetime of experience learning the importance of effort, action, and continuous work. One of his aunts owned a forty-acre farm west of Bartlesville. This farm was a source of many opportunities for challenging work. There, he had endless chores to do. Gardening. Tilling land. Fixing fences. Work on a tractor. Cleaning out the pond. Those are just a few of the things he had to do. It was difficult, dirty, sweat-inducing manual labor.

But after a long day of hard work, my aunt would spoil him rotten as much as she could. That meant being pampered with a meal, maybe a piece of candy, and a whole lot of love. My dad would always talk about how fulfilling it was to be done with the day's exhausting toil so he could reap the rewards. Whenever he recalls those days, he emphasizes that he learned the usefulness of turning effort into reward, of action into consequence.

He didn't really know what he wanted to be when he grew up. He just knew that he wanted to be successful doing it. But first he had to perfect the pattern of turning effort into a reward.

One of the ways my father practiced was by excelling in sports. He didn't mind putting in the effort to maintain his athleticism. He exercised and lifted weights routinely—without a Peloton influencer yelling at him to work harder, mind you. He'd run up, down, and around the solitary hill in town, adorned with a water tower that overlooked everything. He'd run with his friends, but no one could keep up with him.

He ended up playing both football and baseball for his high school and had many professional teams make offers to him. Fun fact: My dad was the very first player to hit a home run at Doenges Memorial Stadium in Bartlesville, *still* the home stadium for the area's high school teams. Out of high school, a variety of teams, including the St. Louis Cardinals, made him an offer to play baseball. But after considering all his options, he decided to pursue football.

It just so happened that the University of Oklahoma had the best football program—by a wide margin—at the time. So it would be no small feat to advance enough in his skill to get a scholarship to that program. But that's exactly the reward that his efforts and actions led to. At that time, the team was coached by Bud Wilkinson, who many considered the best in his profession. My dad played defensive end for Coach Wilkinson, getting after that quarterback with reckless abandon.

But not everything went to plan. As you know from the last chapter, effort and action must be married with the ability to pivot. In my dad's second year, he ended up getting injured. His sports days were over, unfortunately. But he leveraged his scholarship into a college degree. A man of firsts, he was the first person in his family to graduate from college.

He left the University of Oklahoma to attend dental school at the University of Tennessee. From there, he returned to his hometown and set up a dental practice. And as a dentist, he became a successful businessman and helped build his community. He sat on the board of the local bank and established wellness programs for kids. His influence on the community has been felt long past his retirement. And, certainly not least, he was able to provide for his eight kids while teaching us the importance of family.

He was the last Waclaw. And for a time, he was the only Vaclaw. Then my father had five boys. And now he has more than twenty grandchildren who carry his name. So, in no uncertain terms, he staved off the extinction of his name and grew his family legacy.

What my dad's entire life has shown me is that, when you want something, you go get it. You've got to work hard. It isn't handed to you. It's earned. You have a vision, and you can achieve it if you are open to pivoting *and* working hard. Any reward or consequence you're after requires significant effort. It's very much a formula, a repeatable pattern of action. *A* plus

B equals *C*. There's a life balance that brings us what we want, and it's up to us to plug the right things into our own unique equation to get the desired results.

As Stephen Covey once wrote, "I'm not the product of my circumstances. I'm the product of my decisions." That's my father's story. My father taught me to believe that anyone can work themself out of most situations. There is always the variable of luck, but those who put in a lot of effort tend to be luckier. Be flexible. That's important. But you also have to work hard.

ALWAYS BE A STEP AHEAD

When you want to achieve a certain reward or result, effort and action are valuable parts of getting there. But that's easier said than done, right? Brian Tracy's book *Eat the Frog* argues that one way to maintain a high level of effort is to start the day with the most difficult task. After that, Tracy argues, everything else will seem very doable. Not only do you have to put in the effort to work, but you have to put in the effort to work effectively.

While growing up, I, like my dad, worked at the same forty-acre family farm in Osage County, Oklahoma. And the work was gruesomely difficult. Tilling the land. Pulling weeds. Moving logs. Picking green beans. When we were facing down a Saturday of labor, we knew to finish our responsibilities first thing so that we could enjoy the rest of the weekend. I knew to start the morning with the hardest thing so that the rest of the day was bearable.

It had such an effect on me and my siblings that, when we get together, we still talk about it. Instead of watching cartoons on a Saturday morning, we went to work for Auntie Annie, as we called her.

But Auntie Annie would work hard, too. She was probably the hardest worker I have ever met. She lived on that farm well after her husband passed away at a young age and did most of the labor herself, clad in her trademark tube top. She kept that farm thriving and beautiful. Even in her twilight years, when she was battling cancer and undergoing treatment, she worked outside all day. Just a beast of a woman. She was from a line of strong Polish women, and it was quite the sight to see her daily strength even at an old age and infirm.

When the work day was over, she'd stop us at the back door, ready with a bucket of cold water and a washrag. We'd each get our face and neck wiped down before entering the house. She'd have a breakfast prepared, which was always delicious. We'd finish our food with a can of Dr. Pepper she'd keep in her second fridge on the back patio. But it was the tin cans of pudding that we most looked forward to. Yes, canned pudding. These canned treats could be kept on the shelf and needn't be refrigerated. She kept them in her warm pantry, but it didn't matter. We loved those tin-can puddings. She'd serve up the food, refill our cups, and get us anything we asked for. She spoiled us just like she did my father when he was a boy.

We were taken care of, doted on, and rewarded for our efforts—the consequence of hard work. We were kings. And the rewards made the work worth it.

This work ethic has become a vital part of my professional journey. It helped me succeed in graduate school, during my podiatry residency, when I started my own practice, and, of course, in every trial throughout my career that required me to outwork others.

It lingers in me to this day. I make it a point to be the first person to arrive at the office. That helps me get through as many tasks as possible—those can't-be-procrastinated, eat-the-frog tasks—before the chaos of the work day begins.

Doing those tough things first makes one stronger and increases my ability to handle the challenges throughout the day—even those dumpster-fire days where nothing seems to be going right. No one ever worked harder than Aunt Annie. She wouldn't ask any of us to do something she wouldn't do herself. I try to always take the dirty job before asking anyone else to do it. It keeps me a step ahead.

This is where I should probably mention that the slogan of my podiatry practice is "A Step Ahead." It came to me while living in Mexico City. At the time, I would spend days during the week serving in a local mission. This was one of those places where it really did feel like we had to walk uphill both ways to get to our appointments. It was so mountainous. And it was also a very poor part of Mexico City. Homes were built on top of other homes, all boxes of cement. Some homes were painted, but most weren't. Just cement gray as far as the eye could see.

One day I was walking with a companion of mine—a local—and kind of just vented about feeling miserable in the mountain-desert heat and surmounting the steepness of the path and distance to where we needed to go.

With my frustrations shed, I got quiet. Walking side by side in silence, something hit me: I just needed to keep walking. I just needed to put one foot in front of the other and keep putting in the effort. One step at a time, one step ahead. Those in motion tend to stay in motion. And while it would be some time before I became a podiatrist, this aha moment stuck with me. "A Step Ahead."

For my practice, the slogan conveys that our patients aren't getting a standard podiatry experience. They're getting something advanced. Something cutting edge. But it also helps me stay motivated when I see it. It really comes down to always being a step ahead to keep your momentum going. When you keep moving forward, difficult work will get accomplished. Legendary American author Henry David Thoreau phrased it this way: "Success usually comes to those who are too busy to be looking for it."

ENVISION YOUR EQUATION

But working hard for the sake of working hard might not help you achieve the future you want. You don't want to be spinning your wheels. You have to have an end in mind to direct your efforts today. Work backward from your vision or ultimate intention. In other words, don't forget the C in the equation A plus B equals C. When you have a vision of your C, you can plug hard work into A or B and stand a much better chance of achieving what you set out to achieve.

Much like my father wanted to lift himself and his family out of poverty, I knew I wanted to at least maintain the same level of success as my father. I also knew I wanted to become a doctor. And I knew the effort and action it would take to lead to that reward. Going back to Stephen Covey, he pointed out that successful people often begin with the end in mind.[1] So I used that retrofitting to work hard toward becoming a doctor. If you want to achieve specific consequences, think back to the concept of A plus B equals C. What's your C?

When there is a goal in sight—something we'll talk about in more detail in Chapter 7—a human being will work harder and more efficiently to arrive at their desired destination.

---

1 Stephen Covey, *The 7 Habits of Highly Effective People* (Simon & Schuster, 1989).

That's just a fact. And you can use it as inspiration to keep the momentum going when facing your own challenging work.

I learned this, again, while I lived in Mexico. I was put in charge of training a group of young missionaries about aspiration setting. It was my presentation, so I had to come up with something good. It was February and my dad instilled in me a love of football, so I thought of the NFL Combine and all the rigorous tests they put players through.

One of those tests is the vertical jump, where a freestanding pole has little sticks on the side that go all the way up. The player has to stand with their feet shoulder-width apart, jump without any momentum, and then reach to swat the highest possible stick they can. That measures their vertical jump. I didn't have a measurement pole handy, so I pivoted with tape.

Before we got going, I really hyped them up. "You have to jump higher than you ever have before! Really show me what you got!" I used my best Matt Foley motivational speech. One after another, each person in the training jumped and touched the highest point that they could on the wall. We marked off each person's jump with their name on tape. When everybody's turn was over, there was a mosaic forming on the wall.

Then I had them come back and reconsider what they just did. Was that their highest possible jump? Or could they jump higher? The tape on the wall represented a tangible goal—their C. For their previous jump, they had no reference point of what they could achieve. But now they had something to aim for and motivate more effort. I asked them to find their piece of tape, use it as a reference point, and jump higher than the tape, which represented their supposed highest jump.

To a person, every single one of them jumped higher than their previous jump. For some, it was an inch. For others, it was half a foot or more. That's when the lesson became clear to them: We are able to go farther when taking action against a reference point, a defined goal. When we are just arbitrarily doing something—such as living our daily lives—we can't reach our full potential.

When you determine your C, that will help you discover what effort and action—the A and B—can get you there. You can work the equation backward. Start adding up any efforts and actions that will equal those results.

Applying this principle to our professional lives, it would benefit us to start any process with the end in mind. What is it that you want to do? Where do you want to end up? Put that piece of tape up on the wall so that you know where you have to jump beyond.

EFFORT TRUMPS PEDIGREE

Hard work supersedes most things when it comes to being successful.

A lawyer-friend of mine, one day, was telling me about his career path. He became one of the wealthiest and most successful lawyers in the country. But it didn't happen by accident. He started from the bottom and had to work his way up.

He didn't have what would be described as a top-notch pedigree. He didn't come from a family of lawyers. He didn't inherit a firm. The law school he attended is small and relatively unknown. He finished near the bottom of his class.

Coming out of law school, my friend wasn't getting a ton of offers from nationally renowned law firms. But he worked hard to identify a niche within the needs of clients. Shortly thereafter, he became a personal injury lawyer.

It wasn't an overnight success. He had to do the work to build up his clientele first. And he did it well. As he continued to work hard and put the *A* of hard work and the *B* of finding a niche together, the *C* of becoming a top-tier lawyer came into view. Building up his experience through action, he eventually rose to a level where he took on pharmaceutical companies... and won—a reward for his efforts.

Despite his early challenges coming out of law school, he did the difficult work to better himself by adding more effort and action to his equation. And then he strategically adjusted, found a niche, mastered fundamentals, and became one of the most successful attorneys in the entire country. Even though, at one point, he was lagging behind and it seemed like he might not "make it," he kept working. He wanted to stick it out and wait for the tin can of chocolate pudding.

My friend's success came in the form of his profession, but this hard-work-breeds-success principle applies to any part of our lives. It's whatever we define as success for us. The famous story of Rudy Ruettiger comes to my mind as an inspirational example. In the 1970s, the young Rudy had one dream: to play football for the Notre Dame Fighting Irish. That was the definition of success to him. The only real problem was that he didn't have the size (five feet, two inches tall and 165 pounds) or athleticism to earn a scholarship.

At that time, it was the height of Notre Dame's college football fame and prowess. In many ways, that university *was* college football. In other words, he wasn't looking to join just *any* team. And he needed to do what it took to join the best team. In overcoming this challenge, there was nothing he could do about his small stature. But the one thing he did have in his equation was that he wouldn't be outworked.

The first thing he had to do was enroll in the college, but Rudy's application was rejected. To keep himself on the path, he first went to Holy Cross College to get his grades up enough to earn a transfer to Notre Dame. Rudy applied the concept of working hard to achieve. Two years later, Notre Dame accepted him.

But he was only a student, not a player on the sport's premier team. The head coach at the time, Ara Parseghian, allowed walk-on players to try out. One day, Rudy showed up to try out. It was tough work to show he had the mettle to play football, but he earned a spot on the scout team, essentially a practice squad that worked against the starters when running plays and drills. Technically he was on the team at this point, but he didn't get to play in the games. So he kept working hard.

During practice, he'd be going up against the best athletes in the country. And all of them recognized this kid as somebody who worked harder than most. Being on the scout team itself was a full-time job, but how was Rudy going to pay for his education? He worked as a groundkeeper in what little time he wasn't studying or playing football to make ends meet.

Just before Rudy graduated, he was elevated to "dress" for the final football game he was eligible to play in. That just meant he *could* play, not that the coach would let him. He could very well sit on the sidelines for the entirety of the game and miss out on his dream.

The story ends with his efforts paying off. In total, Rudy saw action in three plays that night: a kickoff, an incomplete pass, and a quarterback sack. The quarterback sack was his. Not only did he fulfill his dream of playing, his name will forever appear on the team's stat line as evidence that he fulfilled what he set out to achieve. All due to his hard work and dedication.

At the end of the game, Rudy was famously carried off the field by his teammates to honor what he had accomplished after so many years of continuous dedication. Think about that for a second. Usually a person is carried off the field for the game-winning play in the championship game. In Rudy's case, he made one mundane tackle. But his teammates saw the incredible effort and action Rudy underwent to achieve that accomplishment. He was the first-ever Notre Dame player to be carried off the field and only one of two in history.

To me, Rudy's story is the epitome of setting an aspiration and implementing hard work to achieve it. He knew his C. With that end in mind, he applied the grind, made adjustments, and put in the effort and action to achieve success as defined by him.

When you don't plan your effort and actions around the end results, it is much more likely, in my experience, that (1) you'll waste a lot of valuable time on the way to your success, or (2) you may never achieve high levels of success. Why do I say that? Quite simply, because podiatrists are known to eat their young.

Here's what I mean. The most common path for a podiatrist is to take a job out of residency with an established doctor. For these young associates, most podiatrists will only last in that first job for a short time. I call it the "Three-to-Five-Year Rule." Motivations vary. It could be that they want to go work for another group or doctor. Maybe they want a change of scenery because they don't like the town where they took their first job. Or they want to open up their own practice. Many of us think the grass is always greener somewhere else, and a few short years after starting, we want a different trajectory.

Part of creating success within podiatry is building up a loyal clientele or patient population. Moving locations means starting over from scratch and removing all of the effort and action of those lost years. So, for podiatrists, I recommend they take a job where they can actually, from day one, build the practice and the patient base that will serve them the rest of their career. Make the first question you answer, "Where do you want to live?" Think of what you want your successful practice to look like, and define your C.

And if you're reading this and you're not a podiatrist, you need to find out what success means for your profession compared to where you want to end up (and when). Always figure out what your C is going to be first. From there, continue to work hard to get yourself closer to where you want to be.

CHAPTER 5

THE IMPORTANCE OF DIFFERENTIATION

"The world accommodates you for fitting in, but only rewards you for standing out."

—MATSHONA DHLIWAYO

My children teach me new things every day. And I have six kids, so that's a lot of lessons.

Being a dad is the ride of a lifetime. I love parenting and the challenges it brings. And I want to make sure my kids know that I'm not perfect. Like them, I'm always learning how to be better.

I remember telling my oldest, "Noble, I've never done this before. You're my first child. I'm learning how to raise a son with you." Then his sister came along, and she was a whole different beast…and a whole different parental education. The third came along, and it was another girl! So, I should know what I'm doing this time, right? Wrong, of course! She was as different from her siblings as a pirate from a paralegal.

They learned from me. I learned from them.

One morning with Noble ended up changing both my perspective and my outlook on professional success. He and I were sitting in the car. It was a normal morning, just like any other. I was his ride to school, so I pulled out of the driveway to start our daily routine.

Just as I was going to turn into the street, we got blocked by a big, green garbage truck. "Oh, that's right. It's trash collection day," I said.

The break in action gave us pause. We kind of sat there and watched the garbage guy do his thing. He hoisted up the heavy trash can and dumped it into the back of the truck. We watched the compactor in awe. Fluid sprayed from the filth and ran down the sides of the collection port of the truck. Some of the trash had spilled out, wrappers flapping and viscous liquid slowly rolling down the compactor. A bitter, sulfuric, sweet smell of decaying matter hung in the air, somehow creeping through the door seals of the car.

The garbageman stood back watching before hopping on the back. It didn't look easy for this guy. It didn't look fun. It was clear he had been doing it for several hours that morning, and it was already nearly too early to be awake. Then my son broke the silence. "I could never do something like that for a living. That's gross."

Internally, I reacted in a variety of ways. Part of me agreed. A different part of me saw the value in the work. And part of me—the parent part of me—wanted to help my son explore his thinking to find room for growth and empathy. All of those things quickly combined, and I managed to reply, "You know, son, your dad clips toenails for a living. Really, really gross toenails."

Part of my dad-hope was to convey the importance of not

judging a book by its cover—even if the book has a fantastic cover like this one (kidding). But I moved past that point to explore how *what* we do doesn't really matter as much as *how* we do it. I continued probing him: "How hard is it to become a garbageman? Who is the best garbageman in the world? How do you think one becomes the best garbage collector in the world?"

I posed the idea that it was unlikely that the best garbageman was the one actually collecting the garbage. If they are, then that's just a testament to their work ethic. But, more likely, they mastered their art, worked hard to be better than everyone else, and are now running a business or operation behind the scenes. At parties, they'd likely get a kick out of introducing themselves as being in the garbage business. I concluded by suggesting, "The world's best garbageman is probably in charge of numerous employees and makes good money."

My son understood the point I was trying to make. If you're the best at what you do, you'll be different than the rest who do it. And it is my hope that the experience reframed his idea of me as his dad—walking around and introducing myself, with pride, that I make a living clipping toenails.

Later, when I had time to reflect, I was fascinated by how our experiences can narrativize specific occupations. Various stigmas become attached to certain occupations. Fast-food workers. Garbage collectors. Janitors. Sewage workers. Jobs like these are supposedly undesirable.

Doctors. Professional athletes. Movie stars. Pilots. Jobs like these are not only desirable but respectable, supposedly. But *every* job, if somebody is to be the best or even successful, requires hustle, working hard, mastery, and differentiation.

Just take professional athletes. Very few athletes are able to break through and become professional, let alone successful professional athletes. Around 2 percent of college athletes turn pro. And only 0.00001 percent of high school athletes will make it to the professional level. But then there's Messi, LeBron James, Tiger Woods, Tom Brady, and those best-at-their-job athletes who are plastered on every sports channel on every TV at all hours of the day. We don't see those millions of other athletes who pour their blood, sweat, and tears into their sport only to not make it professionally. We only see the most successful.

But we *do* see all of the garbage collectors who don't transition to the level of company boss. They are everywhere, driving trucks around to collect trash. And we certainly *don't* see the best garbage collector doing interviews on popular podcasts (although that would be fun). So, this kind of thing can create misleading perceptions.

When we only see success, we tend to think of that occupation as glamorous. But there are very few occupations that don't require the unglamorous grind. So, what does that mean, in terms of finding a path to success? The answer, again, is that it's not *what* you do that matters; it's about *how* you do it—and how you endeavor to do it well. Which fast-food company is known for their chicken sandwich? I assume you answered based on how well that company gives you the sandwich as much as how good it tastes. A chicken sandwich is what they do. *How* they do it sticks in your mind.

In my experience, part of doing something well and being successful also requires that you differentiate yourself. You have to make yourself unique to rise through the ranks, to go from high school athlete to Super Bowl champion, or to go from garbage collector to CEO of the garbage collection company.

Differentiation can be achieved through marketing,

growth strategies, or a unique service. It'll depend on your specific occupation. Regardless of method, differentiation can be leveraged to make a real, positive difference in achieving your goals. Just ask Grigory Potemkin.

THE POWER OF POTEMKIN

Standing out means how you present yourself and market yourself. One of the greatest stories in marketing comes from eighteenth century Russia. This era of history contains the famous Potemkin village, which was a fake, portable village created by Grigory Potemkin. These days, as I'm sure you're aware, the phrase "Potemkin village" is used to signify anything that isn't real, is exaggerated, or is in some way a mirage.

So how did "Potemkin village" come to mean this? During the time of Catherine the Great, Russia acquired a region called Crimea from the Ottoman Empire. Potemkin was installed as the governor there, an area that was devastated and left in ruins by a war between Russia and the Ottomans.

There was virtually nothing there, but Catherine the Great knew that there would be lingering battles for the rubble. And if she wanted to maintain it and defend this newly acquired land, she'd have to continue to fight the Ottomans.

But war costs money. In this instance, funds would need to be raised. She invited royals and dignitaries from within Russia and from around the world to visit, see the value of Crimea, and offer funds to help the cause. That's where Potemkin came in.

Catherine tasked Potemkin with wining and dining the dignitaries while acting as part tour guide and part salesman. Part of that meant Potemkin taking everybody down the Dnieper River to view the contested land itself.

Potemkin, knowing the region was devastated, didn't want these dignitaries to think they were chipping in to defend swaths of destroyed cities. He wanted them to see the cultural and economic opportunity that Russia could bring to this area. If, in the dignitaries' minds, Russia could quickly seize an area, build it back up, and make it a thriving community in short order, *that* would be a nation worth investing in.

There was, of course, no time to build the region back up. So he hired actors to pretend to be village people. As far as the villages themselves, Potemkin constructed fake villages. Like early movie sets, they mostly consisted of building facades and were far enough off the river so that nobody could notice their unusability. Flower beds and gardens were added to fill out the reality that the villagers were growing their own crops and using the land to sustain themselves.

As the dignitaries floated down the river, right on cue, the actors would emerge from the buildings and start interacting with the sets as if they were actual inhabitants of the region. Eventually, the boat would pass out of view.

Don't forget…this was a portable village. So, once the dignitaries were gone, the actors would strike the set and move it farther down the river. As the dignitaries approached this "new" village, the actors would once again interact with props and hit their marks.

There's a lot of debate about how exaggerated the Potemkin village stories are, and even more debate about whether or not it actually worked. But the fact of the matter is that the Russians were able to raise money and maintain Crimea for a very long time after that.

Potemkin gave an extremely fascinating story of historical marketing. Of course, Potemkin was creating a false appearance to hide a less favorable reality. When something like that crosses ethical lines, the word "fraud" starts coming into the picture. So I'm not advocating for that, obviously. But there is an important takeaway here: The appearance of success can breed more success.

Another way to think about this concept is the professional adage "Fake it until you make it." It's important to put yourself out there as capable of success and normalize that you can be successful. When you do that, you stand a better chance of actually being successful and achieving success. Providing the highest-quality service, even if barely profitable, establishes your product's reputation. Ask Elon Musk if that worked for Tesla Motors, which struggled to show profits for the company's first decade before becoming the largest EV maker and one of the largest automobile companies in the world.

PERCEIVED SUCCESS CAN LEAD TO ACTUAL SUCCESS

So Potemkin is one thing, but how can we prove the principle of perceived success could work in the modern world? I'll turn to a story involving one of the most successful people I know. He's one of my business mentors, who, like me, married into Texas. He owns hundreds of businesses and started his career as a door-to-door salesman. He revealed one of his differentiation-and-growth strategies to me after I noticed something strange about his car-buying habits.

In his early twenties, his door-to-door sales career was successful enough to allow him to go out and buy a brand-new, luxury Range Rover. It had a refrigerator, vegan leather, and immaculate interior. For his age, it was one of the fancier cars anybody could have.

He only had this car—a dream car for most people—for a few weeks. Then he got rid of it. I'll be honest, for a moment I thought that maybe he had fallen on hard times. But his business, it turned out, was still thriving. There was no way he defaulted on a loan, as he usually paid cash, so I got curious and asked, "Why did you get rid of your new car?"

He explained why he downgraded for a truck. It was a really nice truck, but not as luxurious as the SUV he'd just had. The truck came with everything you can think of. It was raw strength meets high-end comfort.

In terms of *why*, he started on about how a big part of his job was to recruit other salesmen to his team. Prospective salesmen would look to his success as the end result they aspired to have. Only highly successful people could afford the SUV, but most recruits weren't interested in a luxurious SUV. So he had to choose a vehicle that would give off the appearance of success to the aspirations of his recruits. Most middle-aged corporate types might want a Range Rover. But young, college-aged kids would rather have a massive truck.

No one could deny that he was wildly successful, but he strategically meant to appeal to the demographic he wanted to recruit. If they wanted to climb their own ladder to success, he wanted to show them exactly how they could get there by aligning his *C* with theirs. His employees were all men between the ages of eighteen and twenty-five.

When he arrived at the office for the morning meeting, when somebody was with him on a ride-along, or when he made his conspicuous move to head home for the day, he understood that his recruits would notice what he drove. And if *he* was successful—and demonstrated that by owning the dream car that his workforce wanted—these guys would work really hard for him knowing what was achievable.

This strategic alignment of potential, like the Potemkin villages, worked to motivate his recruits and coworkers toward success. My mentor grew his team to one of the largest and most valuable door-to-door companies in US history.

So, like Potemkin, my friend wasn't lying or showing something fake. He bought this truck to demonstrate what was achievable and what he had already achieved. His success was real. But luxury sedans were not something that his workforce would see as valuable. Instead, by acquiring a flashy truck, he influenced real change—and real success—in his workers by simply letting them perceive what was possible.

And it's not just cars. It's how we dress. It's how we walk. It's how we act. It's the environment we create. People place confidence in others who are themselves confident.

There was a study done to determine the attentiveness of kindergarten-aged children.[2] The results showed that when a teacher is perceived as carrying themselves in such a way that can be deemed "attractive," the "students have a greater openness for school activities, the evaluation of the teacher's personality is more positive, the evaluation of the teaching effort is more positive, students expect a higher grade, and the perceived age of the teacher is lower." This study demonstrates it's hardwired human nature to use perceptions to make assumptions. If "attractive" to me is my boss driving a luxury truck, then I'll perceive them positively, trust them more, want to emulate them, participate in the activity of sales, and expect higher compensation.

This basic principle of differentiation through confidence can be applied to any business or profession. That could start with the office or work environment.

In healthcare, the really high-end, competitive, and suc-

---

[2] Marius Marici et al., "The Effect of Attire Attractiveness on Students' Perception of Their Teachers," *Frontiers in Psychology* 13 (2023): https://doi.org/10.3389/fpsyg.2022.1059631.

cessful dentists, plastic surgeons, and medical spas have clinics that look like a fancy palace. There's chic lighting systems complete with a modern chandelier, leather armchairs, fresh water and herbal tea, curated art collections on the walls, pleasant background music, and more. On the other side of the spectrum, when you walk into a dentist's office that looks like the Red Roof Inn, you kind of know what you're paying for.

When I was starting my professional career, I didn't have much to work with. But with the clinics I did open, I tried to be aware of how I could set myself apart through the environment.

I wanted the patients to walk in and feel warm, comfortable, and filled with the feeling that we were effective and successful doctors. So we chose warm, inviting lamplight in favor of cold, sterile fluorescent lights. We painted the walls warm blues and grays instead of stark white. Bright white walls can make people feel empty and lonely, and it adorns the walls of most other medical practices. I installed accessible and comfortable chairs in the treatment rooms, replacing those medical chairs that make the patient feel like a science experiment. I actually had a red carpet that extended from the front door to the check-in for the treatment rooms. I wanted the patients to know that we were there only for them. In every square inch of the clinic, we tried to make a decision that promoted success.

Another great lesson I learned from my father's success was in his private office. He had what I termed the "Wall of Accomplishments." Walking into his private office, you faced a huge wall. It was covered from floor to ceiling in plaques, awards, recognitions, and certifications. There was hardly any exposed wall, and it was an impressive sight. For anybody who walked into his office, you couldn't help but recognize the breadth of everything my father had accomplished. It was more impressive than that episode of *The Office* where Michael

Scott framed and placed behind his desk a "Proud owner of a Seiko Timepiece" certificate.

When it came time for my career, I took his "Wall of Accomplishments" idea and riffed on it a little bit. I thought about my young business mentor and his truck. I thought about the importance of promoting success to breed more success. Just like my dad, I have recognitions and awards, many of which were themselves paid marketing advertisements for "Top Doctors," "Texas' Best Doctors," etc. I would get an email saying that I won some "best of" award and, for $175, I could receive a plaque in my honor. Potemkin village. I've also made paid appearances on television segments as a medical expert. Combined, all of these things helped me stand out from other podiatrists, so I decided to promote those in my clinic to instill confidence in my patients. I pepper some of these materials alongside the art in the waiting rooms and hallways just to let the patients know that they are in good hands—or at the very least that I care about their experience. The more confident they are in my ability to be successful, the more successful I am. Getting others to see you as successful can itself be a success.

And no design element or perception is too small. For example, when I first started, I remember we were required to make a notice visible in the waiting room. The patients were required to see it as they came in. One of my employees Scotch-taped it to the check-in window. It was a teaching moment. I paused and talked with my employee about putting ourselves in the patient's experience. If I walked into a clinic and saw a haggard piece of paper hanging on for dear life by one strand of tape on a closed check-in window, that would send me subtle but powerful messages. It would feel implicitly unwelcoming and create the impression that this clinic is lazy and looks for a quick fix. It might suggest we are the type of clinic that cares more about getting the message out than how we present the message, or cares more than the patient—like the patient is as much of an afterthought as how the notice was hung.

So when it comes to your own work, promote and put yourself out there as successful. Highlight what you do well. When you do, your customers and workers will be confident in what you do. And if you are already giving the effort, flexible enough to pivot, and embracing unglamorous work, then there is very little reason why you shouldn't be able to parlay that confidence into further success.

But the confidence isn't just imbued in others. You'll also help promote self-confidence, which is something I've struggled without throughout my life. Yet, it is important, for motivational purposes, to self-affirm and believe that you have the capacity to do great things.

It's like when you get dressed up to go out. You can put on a tuxedo and do your hair or slap on some sweatpants and put on a grungy hat. When you're dressed to the nines, you feel good about yourself. You've made the effort and you know you're looking at the top of your game. When you wear the sweatpants, you realize you're wearing sweatpants out in public. You're not exactly walking with pride and your chest out.

Caring about how other people perceive you isn't inherently unhealthy. In fact, a little touch of it can help you set and reach a standard. What do you want your standards to be for yourself? Do you want to normalize getting ready for the day in a way that makes you feel good? Or not? The look of success can ultimately help us achieve our vision.

PUT YOURSELF ON A BILLBOARD

Standing out to stand apart, I have found, is a great tool to foster success. By putting yourself out there, the whole community is apt to see you instead of a competitor. Then clients come to you and give you *more* opportunities to demonstrate that you do what you do extremely well.

Don't just sit back idly and hope for the best—that the community will come to you. Why not try to stand out? Why not market yourself? Even if you're the best in town, nobody will know if you don't put yourself out there.

When I was a middle-school-aged kid riding in the car with my dad, we came to a stop at a traffic light. I looked up and saw a billboard on the corner. It was an ad for another local dentist, a competitor of my father. The dentist's face and his big, white smile featured prominently, complete with his slogan and a phone number to set up an appointment.

My first thought was, *How cool would it be to have my dad on a billboard?!* So I asked my dad, "Hey, why don't you have a billboard?" His response still rings clearly in my ears. He offered, "In healthcare, the doctor provides a service. If it's good service, the patients will come to you." I thought that was a noble thing to say, and I let that sink in for a bit before letting it go.

But something about it kept gnawing at me. Over time, I began to wonder if my dad was wrong on this particular topic. Because dental practices were (and are) dramatically increasing in number, promoting oneself seemed like a natural way to set yourself apart from the patients' abundant choices.

My dad was able to maintain his success because he had established a loyal patient base and referral network, but had he started his work one generation later, his practice might not have been able to survive his antimarketing attitude amid the explosion of dental clinics across the industry.

But I understood what my dad was really trying to say. He was a healthcare provider first and foremost. Caring for patients matters before everything else. And that I agree with. Being a doctor is a noble calling. Yet in order to carry out that noble calling, you have to stand out among other providers.

Don't get me wrong. I'm not telling you that you should go out and get a billboard. But I *am* telling you that success can go hand in hand with standing out. What that looks like for you depends on your profession. It could be content marketing, location and market analysis, native content, marketing campaigns, social media advertising, branding, email lists, newsletters, SEO, or billing strategies. It could also simply be stellar service and word-of-mouth reputation. The list goes on. Make it yours.

I learned so much watching my successful father, and I built off of my experience with him. If I wanted to be successful, I had to stand out. That's what I did for over a decade running my own clinics. Now, with Allevio, I'm doing it on a larger scale. We're helping doctors stand out in their market with their individual, unique skillset, like I was able to do in mine. Allevio has become one of the largest podiatry groups in the country, helping many clinics across the country differentiate themselves in order to facilitate more success.

APPLY THE PIVOT

Earlier, I talked about the pivot as being the reaction to getting thrown off course. But it can also be a tool to differentiate yourself. Let me explain.

In podiatry, there was a time when insurances covered medical foot soaks for patients with problematic fungal and bacterial problems. In order to help these patients use the medicine, they would include a small, inexpensive foot spa with the prescription. This provided an enjoyable and very helpful treatment to our patients. Very few podiatrists were implementing these medicines, likely because foot fungus isn't something many get excited to treat! So, to provide the absolute best care to our patients, we would get any patients who qualified using this effective treatment.

Since we were the house-call foot doctors, we were serving a lot of people with fungal toenails or some other dermatological pathology. So, for them, these foot soaks were very, very beneficial to the patient's health. They also felt great and kind of luxurious.

Insurance companies only covered it for a short period of time. Once they don't want to pay for a service anymore, they'll cut reimbursements to the providers, flat-out tell the patients that insurance no longer covers it, or both. So, as a podiatrist, I have to be able to adjust with the times to differentiate our services from our competitors, staying "A Step Ahead" of the competition. We are always looking for the next great treatment available to our patients.

A key differentiator in healthcare is riding the waves of what you can provide to your patients. This "ride the wave" mentality is true for any type of business. Most successful businesses are the ones that continually adapt and follow the trends as they're coming and going. If you don't do that, you won't stand out. Otherwise, a doctor might hit their comfort zone and kind of stay there in a stasis that stifles growth and, more importantly, reduces the quality they provide their patients.

The opposite can also occur when trying to ride the wave of innovation. If you stay on it for too long, it can also stifle growth, which can often lead to a business's death. A fellow podiatrist had this happen to him while riding the wave of amniotic stem cells. If you're not familiar, stem cells are incredibly helpful cells our body produces. These are blank cells that the body can convert into whatever type of cells the body needs, such as helping grow bone, tendons, ligaments, skin, and even organs. With a few exceptions, they can greatly improve almost any pathology.

In podiatry, they have become a great treatment for wounds. Patients with diabetes or neuropathy often develop wounds as they walk around without proper sensation and can literally wear a hole in the bottom of their foot without knowing. These same patients have other health factors that make it very hard for their wounds to heal. So amniotic stem cells have been a popular way to help form layers of skin over an open wound.

The doctor I mentioned implemented these stem cells into his practice around six years ago as they genuinely helped his patients. Because they worked so well, the costs for these products started to climb. When their costs climbed, the reimbursement also went up and became very lucrative. That's when he shifted his business focus to primarily stem cells and wound care. The hyperfocus on one aspect of podiatry (wound care) pushed all other forms of podiatry care, like surgeries and clipping toenails, by the wayside.

These days, reimbursements for these wound-care products have been drastically cut by insurances. Insurances also started changing qualifications and many have started to claw back the payments made to the doctors. This doctor put all his eggs in one basket and wasn't prepared for the wave to crest on this innovation. He was left without the ability to easily pivot.

This doctor's attempt to stand out by using innovative stem cell products blinded him to the rise and fall of certain trends within healthcare. He focused away from innovation and hopped on the popular train too late in the game. He left core podiatry care out of his practice in an attempt to chase profits. He had to either close down his practice or, in order to get back to where he was six years ago, change back to the fundamental bread and butter to create a new business plan that balances riding the industry waves and standing out.

STAND OUT BY STEPPING BACK

Part of standing out is recognizing what you're good at and what you're *not* good at, the topic we'll cover next. To help a business stand out, find somebody who knows how to do the things you're not good at really well. Let specialists implement their specialty.

If there's anybody reading this who needs brain surgery, don't hire me. But if you need your toenails clipped, I'm your guy. I often joke with people that, in an apocalyptic event, all I'll be able to contribute to the remnants of society is to clip everybody's toenails. I'm really, really good at it. Doesn't matter if they're normal, big, old, or eagle claws. I can do it. It's important to recognize what we do well.

But it's also equally important to recognize what others do better. And I've noticed that the strongest businesses are filled with people who have strengths that complement each others' weaknesses.

CHAPTER 6

LEVERAGING THE STRENGTHS OF OTHERS

"If you are the smartest person in the room, then you are in the wrong room."

—CONFUCIUS

I've often faced the consequences of thinking, *I could do that.*

One summer, as part of installing a backyard playground for my kids, somebody gave me the advice of putting synthetic turf down underneath the playground. I liked that idea. It was a softer surface for my kids, was green year-round, reduced ants and other bugs, and it would be easier to maintain.

I hired a professional landscaping company. They were legit. They ripped up the grass and topsoil, removed all the debris and mulch, took down part of a wood retaining wall, cleaned everything up, put down different layers of crushed rock and sand, unrolled the turf into its final position, and then fastened the turf down with huge staples. It was impressive and really fun to watch.

After the crew left, I surveyed the scene. That's when a thought intruded: *I could do that.*

I hope, so that I'm not alone, that that's a very common reaction. Certain husbands all over the world are guilty of looking at a broken toilet handle, a power socket that's not working, or a hole in the drywall and announce to the family like a wannabe hero, "I can totally fix this. No need to worry!"

And then, after whatever was fixed, everyone in the family would be clapping in celebration and gratitude each time we entered a room. They would say, "There he goes! That's the guy who fixed our sink. I'm so proud to call him my husband. He can do anything!"

So there I was, looking at this pristinely installed turf. I started scanning the rest of the yard, and I noticed one little spot surrounded by trees that had been the bane of my existence since we had moved in. I take a lot of pride in keeping my grass green, but I could never really get this little corner to produce thick, plush grass. It was just out of reach of the nearest sprinkler and had too little sunlight to grow grass. So how could I fix this? I decided it was time to convert it into a little turf putting green.

I could do that.

First stop, the hardware store. And this was no job for a standard shopping cart. Instead, I grabbed one of those heavy-duty platform trucks. I piled on what YouTube said was the proper amount of inexpensive turf, bags of crushed granite, bags of sand, and a shiny new shovel, and brought all of this stuff to the corner of the yard.

The spade broke ground, and off I went. I started going through the whole process of removing debris and then layering the rock and sand. The company I hired needed a dozen men. And here I was, just one guy. *Not bad*, I thought, assuming that the sunlight was illuminating the color of my eyes and glinting off my sweat in a movie-star kind of way.

At some point, the realization came over me that I was in way over my head. As progress continued, I had too much crushed granite but not enough sand. That was another trip to the store. I began again, and how I was laying the turf down just didn't look quite the same as the professionals. I kept cutting it short and had these leftover pieces I couldn't do anything with. That meant another trip to the store for turf.

Weeks, not days, later it got done eventually. It took me much longer and cost me a lot more than what the landscaping company quoted. And that's time I'll never get back. In seven years, I've probably used the putting green three times.

After all the toil, I actually did learn a valuable lesson, one that was worth the mistake of installing the green myself. We all have our strengths and weaknesses. We don't need to do everything. Next-level growth often means delegating to other experts to help lift you up in areas where you could use the help.

If somebody can do something better, cheaper, and quicker, leverage their professional skills as part of your own growth. In my podiatry practice and now with Allevio, I have surrounded myself with people who are better within their sphere of expertise than I would be.

In my experience, many of my fellow doctors are doing a lot of things themselves. They're the ones on the phone with the IRS, ordering supplies, doing payroll, managing the budget, training the staff, researching cost-saving measures, doing their own billing, ensuring compliance, and more. I've watched these doctors struggle and suffer. The truth is, they're not getting as superior of a product while also taking time and energy away from doing what *they are good at*. In the end, that lessens revenue and stifles growth.

If you are good at clipping toenails for a living, clip toenails. Don't try to do your own taxes, too. If you are good at restoring cars to their original condition, do that. Don't refocus your efforts toward billing. And the same is true for any profession you are pursuing.

Surround yourself with the people who are smarter than you in the ways your business can be smarter. Doing it all yourself might lead to worse results. And although specialists might seem like a significant up-front cost, they usually generate revenue that ends up being multiples of what they cost.

THE WHOLE IS GREATER THAN THE SUM OF ITS PARTS

Here's another way to think about how fantastic the results can be from stepping back and delegating to specialists.

Music has always been a big part of my life. I remember my mom and brother would play John Denver songs together while my brother played the guitar or piano. I loved watching them create beautiful music that filled our home. It really inspired me to learn how to play, too.

I was around thirteen years old when I started to learn to play guitar, bass, and drums, and to sing. I also developed a love for writing songs. My first band was really just my high-school buddy and me. We wrote our own songs. He played the drums, and I played guitar. We had a lot of fun and developed a musical hobby together.

When I got to college, a couple of my roommates were into playing music. We formed a six-person band, and all of us took turns writing the songs we would play. As far as college bands go, we enjoyed mild success. I played guitar and sang. Others played rhythm or lead guitar, drums, and the keyboard. Six different people, multiple different instruments.

We were all talented in our own ways, but the success we had was because, as a team, we were awesome bandmates. If you plucked one of us out and put us in a room, playing our instrument by ourselves, it would still sound really good. Everybody sounded fantastic on their own—great soloists. But when we got together, that's when we created music.

Music is inspirational and life-changing. So when you put us all into the same space and we played in unison, magic happened. When you combine the efforts of many talented people, you can create something more spectacular than you ever could on your own.

What's more, it wasn't my forte to play the piano—at least not well. So what made us a good band was the skill of getting somebody better than me (and the others) to play piano. Then I could focus on singing, another bandmate could focus on bass, and so on. It's just like my practice. I *could* do the billing, accounting, or marketing. Or, I could hire people who are better at that than me so I can focus on clipping toenails.

I'm lucky enough to have continued playing music after college. One day in my late thirties, I was at my church gym playing basketball when a couple of guys came in thinking they'd find microphone stands there. Interested, I started looking with them. We found them, and then they took me to a room with a full set of drums, guitars, and amplifiers. We just started jamming. Then they asked me to sing something. For the next four years, every Thursday night after basketball, we would play music. That led to post-jam Whataburger and long-lasting friendships.

Part of the joy in playing music is contributing to something larger than yourself. You can add the bass, the lead, the voice, or the percussion to help make a group shine.

What was important in that endeavor, though, was doing what worked best for the band. I could play the keyboard, but I'm not trained. I can bang sticks on drums, but I wasn't as good as our band's drummer. Playing good music is about getting the best person at a specific instrument in a position to play that instrument.

When good musicians play together, the whole ends up being greater than the sum of its parts. I find that something similar occurs in my professional life. There's a reason why people say, "Let's work in concert." Like music bands, businesses thrive when everybody is playing their part and employing their expertise to complement the other moving parts.

Sure, I could do the accounting and billing for my practice. But just because I *can* doesn't mean it would be the best thing for my practice. There are people out there that are better at it, can do it faster than me, and can do it cheaper than me.

From that philosophy—and when I surrounded myself with people who are more highly specialized at what they do than I am—my practice ended up growing, becoming more successful, and helped more members of the community maintain their health.

PEOPLE CAN LIFT YOU UP OR BRING YOU DOWN

Jim Rohn famously said, "You are the average of the five people you spend the most time with." For me, Rohn reveals more than just what's possible if you surround yourself with smart people. He's also cluing us in to what will happen if we don't.

If you surround yourself with people with objectively

growth-inhibiting traits—people who are always late, negative in their attitude, impulsive, arrogant, dishonest, unreliable, apathetic, manipulative, lazy, close-minded, inflexible, narcissistic, passive-aggressive, or who never take responsibility and only blame others—those traits tend to rub off on you. We accept those traits as being a "normal" part of the human experience. So, if you are not taking into account the people you surround yourself with, you have a glaring gap in your unique recipe to success that you need to more thoughtfully complete.

And when you go to fill in that part of your success recipe, surround yourself with people who are better than you. It will normalize being a better, growth-oriented person. You'll want to be a better person. You'll stand a better chance of putting in the effort and action to make that happen.

I've been lucky in that my closest allies growing up were my siblings and family members. Since I'm the second youngest, it gave me the opportunity to be around and kind of observe them all grow into their personal and professional lives to find success. Each did it in their own way that was unique to them. Whatever they did, they did it well. When it comes to my own medical practice, I give them a lot of credit for the success I've found.

And I've also had a lot of help outside of my family. When I started my practice right out of residency, I essentially had no idea what to do. I had one employee. When the first patient arrived, my lone employee looked at me and said, "Um... where's the New Patient paperwork? Your patient needs to fill that out." I looked at her with a blank stare. I had no idea I needed paperwork for new patients. Luckily, my employee, having experience and being smarter at administrative duties than I was, was able to whip something up quickly to use. And ever since then, I've been constantly trying to find someone better at doing things than I am. It helps me either learn, mirror their skill, or pull them in to leverage their expertise. As I've grown professionally, I continue to surround myself with people like her to help me run my business.

If you took a snapshot of the most successful people, it's likely that the bulk of them didn't achieve their success on their own. Instead, they will have surrounded themselves with talented people who helped them along the way—people whose strengths complemented their weaknesses.

To illustrate this point, I want to turn to Steve Jobs. I know, I know. People love talking about Steve Jobs. But usually the conversation is about his status as a visionary and leader and those sorts of things. What is not often discussed is his ability to find the right people and plug them into the right places.

When you start looking at Steve Jobs's supporting cast, anyone can quickly recognize that it's a who's-who of iconic names. Let's just look at a few. Jobs's Apple co-founder is none other than Steve Wozniak, also known as Woz. He is a technical genius who co-engineered the first Apple computers, the Apple I and the Apple II. He also helped engineer the technology for universal remote controllers. Without Woz, there is no Jobs.

Jobs was a visionary, yes, but he wasn't an artist. Jony Ive is the artist and designer responsible for the look of most of Apple's products, including that iconic 1990s iMac, the iPod, and, later, the iPhone. Ever felt in awe of the futuristic look of an Apple Store? That was Jony Ive's design work. Again, Jobs gets all of the credit, but without the work of Ive, the pockets of the world would house a much different-looking device. Would it have been as successful without Ive's design?

To round it out, we would be remiss not to mention Tim

Cook, whose business acumen and operational efficiency helped scale Apple globally. Jobs is good on a stage and as the poster child of the company, but without an actual business plan, not much can get accomplished. That's where Cook came in, helping transform Apple into a global brand.

Steve Jobs was smart for accumulating talent. And he understood that his success came not from doing everything himself but from building a team of exceptional individuals who complemented his weaknesses. *That* is a lesson we can take from Jobs.

And although I was lucky to be born into a family with amazing siblings whom I could look to for inspiration, it's a different beast when it comes to employees. I had to find, pick, learn from, sometimes train, and possibly replace my own employees. If you run a small business, you get to *choose* your employees. Choose wisely.

HIRE FOR CHARACTER AND POTENTIAL OVER QUALIFICATIONS

Surrounding yourself with good people in business usually involves hiring people. When I started building my practice, I was looking for that champagne taste on a whiskey budget. Financially, there was only so much I could do, so I wanted to do the best with what I could afford.

When you put in the effort to hire well, it will pay dividends later. That has been true for me. For example, one of the key people I hired early who is still with me today is Kim Clark. Before she came to work for me, she worked at a call center where I was outsourcing callouts, appointment making, and answering the phone.

There wasn't enough room in my first building for somebody doing Kim's work. I was subleasing basically a closet-sized room from another doctor.

That first year, when I would regularly collect patient feedback on what was going well and how I could improve, *all* my patients—coming to the office or receiving house-call service—reported their satisfaction with Kim. One comment was, "Just the best voice." "She's so great!" "She has a bright personality!" "She's super friendly." "I just think the world of her."

My immediate thought was, *Who's Kim?* I didn't have anybody on my payroll by that name. Then I put two and two together. I reached out to the call center and asked that all my patients be directed *only* to Kim.

Kim herself, I found out later, had fallen on hard times. She had recently gone through a rough personal patch, and, in the midst of fighting for those things, lost her promising corporate career. A job at a call center was the only thing she could get. Making everything even worse, the call center she worked at was slated to close down.

She had been answering our calls for two years at that point. So I asked her, "Why don't you come work with us?" She agreed and came on board to answer our phones. She was so incredibly good at her job that she was very obviously retaining and adding high-value patients, which helped me grow the practice.

I hired her for her character and contribution, but I also saw her potential. Because of her experience in the corporate world, she was actually awesome at a bunch of things. There were few instruments she couldn't play in the concert that was my practice. After a little bit of time, I put her in charge of managing all of the house calls. Then I promoted her to office manager. She had three employees working for her. As we added additional clinics, she became the corporate manager of the clinics, training and managing the office managers at each location. Today, Kim continues to work on the corporate side of the Allevio organization.

Not only did she thrive in teaching the staff how to do the protocols and uphold all of the business elements of the work, she also brought the culture—the culture that was evident in that initial run of patient feedback. She brings that welcoming and bright attitude we try to embed in every aspect of the work.

I can say with confidence that there is no way that I ever could have gotten to where I am today without Kim. She is my living proof that hiring well and surrounding yourself with good people can skyrocket your success. And it's a mutual success.

What's worth emphasizing is that Kim, on paper, might never have had a traditional opportunity to break into healthcare. If she had put her CV in front of any clinic, it would have been flatly rejected. Her on-paper "qualifications" weren't there. So she wouldn't have had a traditional opportunity.

But my patients recognized her character and her strengths. And that helped me see her potential and how valuable she would be to any business. At that point, her CV didn't matter to me because I knew the type of employee she was, and that she was good at her role.

She's also a good person. To me, being a good person is a superior trait. Kim is an example of that. And so is Krystal Lovos. Krystal started out as an entry-level, front desk employee. Very quickly after she was hired, another employee came to me complaining that she wasn't doing her job. The complaint I got was a little more venomous than that, actually.

The one thing I knew about Krystal was that she was super friendly, always positive, was easy to smile and laugh, and asked everybody about their day. After a back-and-forth with the complainants, I looked into her performance. What was in the complaints wasn't there in reality. There wasn't anything she didn't know. Maybe there was a learning curve at first, but she caught on quickly.

What I did note from my review of her was that she wouldn't just welcome patients into the office, she'd remind them about important information, would ask about grandkids, and very clearly cared about our patients. I had no doubt in my mind that her style was likely *the* reason many of our patients were coming in to see doctors.

Since that time, she's climbed up in my company and is in my inner circle. Now she's a huge component to our house call scheduling and training. To me, somebody like Krystal is a good example that when someone is a good person and has personality traits that enhance their job performance, it's likely that they'll contribute to the growth of a company.

If you're looking through a stack of résumés and CVs, you can't discern whether or not the applicant is a good person. It's not a traditional "qualification" that a company would ask for. But hiring people like Kim and Krystal, based on character and potential, has always helped me achieve success. Character and potential are underserved metrics that small-business owners might want to take into account when hiring smart people.

"SAVING A BUCK" IS EXPENSIVE

In business, it's easy for us to think we can save a buck by doing a job ourselves. That thinking, though, is wrong more often than it is right (if it's ever right). It's worth repeating: If you can find somebody who can do something better, cheaper, and faster than you, those are people who can help your business grow.

You can't play all of the instruments at the same time to make music. Johann Wolfgang von Goethe famously said, "Tell me with whom you associate, and I will tell you who you are." The people you surround yourself with *will* inspire you. They *will* rub off on you. You *will* become like them. So make sure, in your profession, that you choose those people well. Let them lift you up, the way an ensemble of guitars, drums, voices, and keyboards lift each other up to make music.

Having a team like this will keep you inspired to be the best at what you do. Inspiration is vital to growth. Make it a goal of yours to start surrounding yourself with the best people.

CHAPTER 7

THE USEFULNESS OF DISCOMFORT

"The way I see it, if you want the rainbow, you gotta put up with the rain."

—DOLLY PARTON

Let's talk about Rocky Balboa and Ivan Drago.

Rocky is an iconic American film character only slightly less famous than the amazing training montages that appeared throughout the *Rocky* series.

In perhaps the most remembered film in the series, *Rocky IV* (1985), which was released near the tail end of the Cold War, Rocky was pitted against a Soviet opponent named Captain Ivan Drago (played by Dolph Lundgren). Drago happened to be a captain in the Soviet Army and, as the training montage revealed, used unnatural means to prepare for his bout with Rocky. Drago was a fearsome opponent. Rocky embraced the discomfort of the challenge. Meanwhile, Rocky did things au naturel by lifting up big bags full of stones, chopping wood, growing a beard, and using a length of farm rope as a makeshift jump rope. And all of this happens while we get to listen to "Heart's on Fire" by John Cafferty. It's fantastic.

But it's also inspirational. In each of the *Rocky* films, Balboa has a clear goal he's working toward by beating a specific opponent. Everything he does in the middle of the film is the work he does to meet a larger goal.

During that training montage in *Rocky IV*, there's one shot that shows Rocky has placed a photo of Drago in a mirror to remind him of the goal he has in front of him. That's an important moment, and it tells us that, for Rocky, it's not just about lifting rocks and chopping wood and growing a beard. He was doing those things for a reason—to defeat Drago—and he needed to keep that reason at the top of his mind. By having a vision and reminding himself of that achievement, he was staying inspired to work hard.

My experience in business isn't too dissimilar to Rocky, in terms of setting a challenge to push me a little out of my comfort zone and maintain a growth trajectory. The discomfort that comes with a challenge generates motivation. When they work in tandem, anyone can achieve more than they could before.

Part of success is being inspired and staying inspired. Challenging yourself is one way to keep a vision of your future top of mind, inspiring you to do what's needed to get the reward and consequence you're after.

A SLAM DUNK

For the last few years I have had a colleague who ended up being highly influential on me. It seemed like he would set his mind to something and accomplish it with ease. The more and more I watched him, the clearer it became that he was always using discomfort to challenge himself, grow, and achieve new things.

Since he was in high school, he'd have a journal with lists of personal challenges like, "Surpass 100 yards receiving in a football game this season. Read one book outside of school every month." Things like that. Then he'd go out and do them. Over the years, when I'd reach out to him, I was pleased to learn that he still challenged himself in this way. He was older, so the challenges would be more family or professionally oriented. But by giving himself something difficult to strive for, he was able to maintain more consistent success in achieving them.

But what makes a challenge achievable? Well, just that. It needs to be within reach and possible.

It's always been a dream of mine to dunk a basketball. But is it realistic and achievable? I'm five foot eight, a little porky, and in my forties. There's a low probability that I'd be able to dunk a basketball on a regulation hoop. I'm not saying I couldn't do it, but the amount of work it would take is not aligned with my current priorities.

So what's the takeaway? *The less achievable the challenge, the more exponentially difficult the work will be in achieving it or growing beyond it.*

Challenges need to be realistic. We all want to climb the proverbial Mount Everest, but if we have a hard enough time just going up the stairs in our house, we need to start smaller. Start with simpler challenges, and then as you achieve them slowly you can build toward bigger and bigger challenges that, because of the foundation you've built, become a slam dunk.

Early in my practice, I challenged myself to see ten patients in a day. Then, once I achieved that, it was fifteen patients. Then twenty. Each time I prioritized maximizing patient care.

After that, I wanted to grow the business enough to add an associate doctor. With that accomplished, I wanted to generate $100,000 in revenue. I did just that. After a series of similar challenges, revenue kept going up until it got into the millions. From there, I pivoted to opening multiple clinics. Sometime after that, it all led to me selling my practice.

In that journey of incrementally uncomfortable challenges, I set small, achievable objectives that, once accomplished, led to a larger achievable vision. In other words, I couldn't go simply from residency to selling a practice. I had to set and achieve incremental challenges along the way.

COMFORT KILLS PROGRESS

Now that I've insisted that success comes when you set achievable challenges to get outside of your comfort zone, let me offer a big, fat caveat: Don't create "challenges" that are *too* easy. There is a sweet spot. Anything that can be achieved without much effort or thought leads to complacency, stagnation, and the death of growth.

In my own practice, for example, I had established a system that became very automated. I brought in the right people to run the clinics, care for the patients, and promote steady growth. My system became self-reliant. I had skilled people like marketers, IT, legal and accounting, human resources, development strategy, and regulatory professionals to handle it all for me. That steadily allowed the practice to grow year over year.

It was a situation where compounding, replicating success had been set into motion without me having to do much more. Superficially, that sounds amazing, right? In reality, it was much different.

I was so comfortable in my life that hobbies and other interests started shifting my focus away from podiatry. I was dabbling in real estate investment. I put more of myself into breeding animals like miniature Highland cows and opened the equestrian center. Those parts of my life are still amazing, don't get me wrong. But these little distractions contributed to a bigger problem: complacency. These hobbies and interests weren't the problem; it was the autopilot I put myself on. I started putting less thought and effort into my own practice. What I had devoted my educational and professional life to was now just a place I worked at a few days each week. I didn't recognize that I was on a continual journey of growth.

Comfort can be the enemy of progress. My podiatry business was stalling. I was no longer a rolling stone but a rock stuck in the mud of complacency and comfort.

Too much comfort. It was in this abundance that I started battling depression. It was very hard on me, my wife, and my family. I've gone my whole life with anxiety, and yet I've always been extroverted and loved social interaction. My depression drew me away from friendships. I dropped many of my hobbies like music and sports. A dark feeling of hopelessness started creeping into my life. I had accomplished nearly everything I had set out to accomplish professionally, but I was also the lowest I had ever felt. What I came to realize was that I had gotten comfortable. And it was a comfort zone I didn't really want to get out of.

The work ethic my Aunt Annie had instilled in me was replaced with a "worry-free and carefree" apathetic viewpoint. I remember telling a close friend around the New Year that it was my intention to *not* set any goals or challenge myself for the next year. So I stopped growing through the discomfort of achieving new things. I ate whatever I wanted, including Blow

Pops, Pop-Tarts, and other empty foods. My daily workouts continued but had no structure. Ipso facto, I started gaining weight.

I wouldn't commit to invitations. Friends would invite me to do things, and I would just say, "No." I didn't like making plans. I deliberately avoided people and spent my time alone or with my animals. Even that didn't give me joy. Too many interactions with my kids and wife were perceived as negative; I thought I was messing up as a father and husband. Then I felt ashamed and guilt-stricken, which only amplified everything.

It was like, because I stopped trying to improve, my life atrophied. The concept of muscle atrophy is that without the constant, consistent cycle of repetitive use, our muscles will eventually break down and the body will seek to destroy muscles in order to use them for energy.

When we *do* use our muscles, we are breaking bonds within the cells—the molecules and muscle fibers. This breakdown requires our bodies to repair the bonds in order to rebuild and regrow the muscle tissue. That process of rebuilding actually builds the muscle back better and stronger. Notice the pattern here. In order to grow, a muscle must first be broken, challenged to seek regrowth, and then build itself back stronger than before. The exact same thing is true for growing your life through self-progress and goal setting.

My mental health broke down and I got complacent when I was on autopilot and stopped challenging myself. I noticed, too, that this complacency coincided with a time in my life where I wasn't setting goals, endeavoring to grow, or setting myself in motion to move forward. I was stagnant. And because of that, I was actually moving backward. What this reveals is that we need to challenge ourselves—make ourselves a little uncomfortable—in order to keep growing and moving forward. Your ambitions should be realistic and achievable, but they should also be a little challenging.

What it comes down to is the fact that success is not a landing platform. Success is a process of always setting another goal, creating a new challenge, and seeking out consistent growth. Challenging, slightly uncomfortable goals can become that mountain that we can conquer. That motivation to keep us moving, one step at a time.

GROW THROUGH DISCOMFORT

When you challenge yourself, make yourself a little uncomfortable. That discomfort can push us to our limits and stretch our abilities. Challenges need to be "do one hundred push-ups" and not "do ten push-ups." Many people could probably do like thirty-five push-ups. But once they get around the one hundred mark, that's probably going to hurt. That'll ensure some discomfort and soreness for a few days.

A friend of mine had the habit of carrying hundred-dollar bills with the intention of giving them out to folks. I noticed that he'd even give them to strangers if he felt they did something kind or were in need. That is a large amount of money for most anyone. I didn't understand why he specifically did that amount. I'd ask him, "Why don't you do this with something smaller, like twenty dollars? That would still be really generous."

His answer struck me. He said, "I give them a hundred dollars more for myself. It hurts. It's hard. I could have used that money elsewhere. But by giving them this amount, I am truly giving something that is challenging to give up." He was telling me that he was creating a situation outside of his comfort zone. For my friend, he wanted his sacrifice to be sufficient enough that it wasn't easy to do. He wanted it to be a very deliberate and intentional act that wasn't easy.

This was one way he kept himself uncomfortable. And that discomfort—one created out of his generosity—helped him find ways to grow and avoid complacency both personally and professionally. I should note that he's been handing out this money since he was in college (and, like most people in college, strapped for cash), and he's still doing it today, having used this strategy to help motivate the growth of his professional success.

UNCLE WALT

Speaking of somebody who grew through discomfort, Walt Disney—or "Uncle Walt" as he was known on the TV program *Disneyland*—knew the importance of channeling a challenge to create growth.

He faced an early challenge when he lost the rights to his first popular character, Oswald the Lucky Rabbit. Not only that, but he was fired from his position as spearheading new Oswald cartoons. On his train ride back to California, Disney sat in that discomfort and used it as motivation to create the most famous cartoon character in history, Mickey Mouse.

Additionally, using goals as part of a growth and success-building process defined his entire career. His first goal was to innovate live-action short comedies by overlaying animated characters, as he did in the *Alice Comedies* (1923–1927). From there, he set a goal to create sync-sound animation and master the commercial art of animated shorts. He did that with Mickey Mouse in *Steamboat Willie* (1928).

Notice that when Disney became successful, he didn't get complacent. It didn't stop him from setting new goals. Was he going to be happy with the stasis of making Mickey Mouse shorts for the rest of his life? No. Why? Because he understood that a sustainable approach to success is creating discomfort through setting new challenges. That's when Disney turned to the possibilities of feature-length animation, which, up until that time, was not commercially viable.

Animation was an expensive business. It took hundreds of artists many years. That requires paying a lot of salaries for quite a while without any revenue coming in.

But Disney had a vision. And he invested in himself (and his business) to achieve that vision. He hired the best animators at top dollar and helped guide their creativity. The result was 1937's *Snow White and the Seven Dwarfs*. It was a smash hit. And the money he earned paid for his new studio in Burbank, California. The films he went on to make there are not just some of the most beloved American movies ever, they also led to him becoming the most successful Academy Award winner to date, with twenty-six total.

Bursting with success, he was done dreaming big, challenging himself, and growing, right? Wrong. He continued to push boundaries and get out of his comfort zone. While at a park with his kids, he watched them ride on a kiddie merry-go-round. Not able to join them, he sat on a bench to watch and, as he later recalled, thought to himself, *There ought to be a place where the kids and parents can have fun together.*[3] By the summer of 1955, that thought became Disneyland.

He meticulously planned every aspect of Disneyland, setting clear objectives for the artistic design, attractions, atmosphere, and guest experience. He had to train his own people and founded what's now called Imagineering, more

---

3   Walt Disney, "Walt's World," interview by Fletcher Markle, *Telescope*, CBC, September 25, 1963, television, 30:35.

or less inventing a new branch of entertainment artistry. Walt even put his house as collateral when trying to finance Disneyland. That challenge and discomfort fostered the will to get it right, and Walt Disney revolutionized (and perhaps invented) the theme park industry. While I'm not endorsing that everybody should put their house up for collateral, I'm simply using it as an example that discomfort can pay off.

Today, Disney Parks are the most successful branch of the Disney Company. But at that time, Walt Disney was putting himself in a difficult space. He borrowed $17 million to build Disneyland ($220 million in 2025). That included doing a deal with ABC to televise a program—called *Disneyland*—to drive ad revenue to pay back ABC, one of his creditors.

Unfortunately, Disney died early due to lung cancer, a disease caused by a life of smoking. Up until he died, he was still working on new challenges. For example, his vision of what became Walt Disney World was wildly different from the end result. (The park itself opened after he died.) His real goal was to create an experimental prototype community of tomorrow—EPCOT. It wasn't a theme park; it was an actual city. Disney had moved on from theme park design and set himself new goals as a city planner to try and help humanity become more efficient and help challenges facing modern cities. Unfortunately, he didn't live to complete his last dream. And when he died, the company didn't have the financial means (nor any charismatic leader) to continue the process of pursuing his last big goals.

Disney always sought growth, which built a path from Mickey Mouse to urban planning. In his life, Disney didn't just hope for success. He set ambitious goals and pursued them relentlessly. He created an entertainment empire that still thrives today.

But, of course, there aren't that many Walt Disneys. It's not every day that we can use discomfort to set world-changing goals, meet them, grow, set new goals, and continue that upward trajectory. For most of us, we fall off the horse a time or two. Discomfort can feel like or lead to failure.

GET BACK ON THE HORSE

Famed British leader Winston Churchill wrote, "Success is stumbling from failure to failure with no loss of enthusiasm." Sometimes, you can challenge yourself and fail. That's okay. That's part of the process.

A life-lesson analogy to draw here could come from football. When a receiver drops a pass that hit them right in the chest, that can be a momentum-killing moment. *Everything* else had been executed perfectly. The offensive line set up great blocks. The quarterback dropped back, went through their progression of reads. The running back chipped the oncoming lineman. And the quarterback fired the pass off to the open receiver. Then the last part of the sequence—the receiver making the reception—cost the team valuable yardage. And that kind of drop is demoralizing. It's easy for a team to keep spinning their wheels after that.

So how does the team course correct? Most times, the coach will call a play that goes right back to that receiver, usually a smaller or simpler play. The purpose of it is to get the ball back in the receiver's hands as quickly as possible so that the receiver gets back into the rhythm of success. And perhaps more importantly, the entire team witnesses that success and trusts that they can continue to build small successes into the *big* success, which is winning the game.

In football, where there's a failure, it's important to dust yourself off and try again with the same gumption as before.

The same process is at play with riding a horse. When you get bucked off, you should immediately get back on. This shows the horse that it's not okay to do it, and it helps the rider get over any potential fear of falling again. Of course, what they don't tell you is that when you get bucked off, it's really scary. I am not known to be the best rider in our family, but I am easily the best when it comes to falling off a horse. I have mastered this art.

One of the hardest falls I've ever had came from a horse appropriately named Shiner, a white-paint quarter horse with blue eyes. We used him primarily for hunting and jumping. Anytime I'd ride him, I'd have to constantly pull his head back straight because he'd be looking for downed trees or a bush to jump over.

I wasn't quite aware that you shouldn't ever let a horse reach full speed since they're really hard to stop once they get going. So, to summarize, I was going top speed on a horse that loved jumping. We were chugging along and then, all of a sudden, I was up in the air. Seemingly just as quickly, I hit the ground. The first thing I saw when I looked up was the horse coming down on top of me. Thankfully, I was able to roll away at the last moment. (Like I said, I have a talent for falling off horses!)

But when Shiner and I dusted ourselves off, I got right back on him and just walked. I stayed on that horse for another two hours. It wasn't for the horse; it was for me. Getting back on him and normalizing our partnership helped me quell the fear of being bucked. When you think about it, riding a horse at walking speed for two hours doesn't sound like an important goal. But it was for me at that moment. Sometimes using small, achievable challenges to overcome the lost momentum of something you failed to achieve can keep you on the path to success as you set and seek to achieve your bigger vision.

EMULATE YOUR HEROES

In my life, I've found that those I want to emulate most have helped me learn the importance of growing through discomfort. Going back to the last chapter, if you surround yourself with good people, you should be able to see what they are doing in their lives that you can replicate. They're successful people. It's okay to copy them.

Be thoughtful enough to notice both the big things *and* the small things that generate success for these individuals in your life. What's an example of a small thing, you ask? One of the most successful people I know—and also a close friend—was chatting with me in his office. I noticed that, behind him, there was a little beverage refrigerator. I paused and thought, *What a great idea to have something on hand in a pinch*. When I inquired further, he explained that it was there so that he could offer people a soda, water, or whatever they might want. It was a way for him to set himself apart from others—to offer an extra service that few others did.

So I did that in my office, too. If one of my incremental challenges for my clinic was to create a warm and welcoming environment, offering beverages to anybody coming into my office was one small way of succeeding. And, when combined with all of the other small successes, it adds up to big successes.

I've found that emulation in this way is a perfect strategy for challenging oneself and growing through discomfort. As you go to implement this same strategy, keep in mind that your heroes can be anybody. They can be your parents, siblings, friends, or public figures. As long as they offer you value by revealing strategies on how to challenge yourself, they're the right heroes to target.

For me, the people I wanted to emulate first and foremost were my father and siblings. They've all achieved success and in their own unique ways. And they've done it the right way. They're excellent spouses, parents, and people. So there's nothing wrong with wanting to play copycat when the trait you're copying is successful.

Think of it like an informal apprenticeship system that you are responsible for. Like a residency program that you run. In residency, doctors train underneath another doctor. Residents are constantly witnessing how things are accomplished by the more experienced doctors. Use the same frame of mind when looking at your heroes. Learn how successful people are doing it to set your own standards and goals.

ACHIEVABLE, REALISTIC, AND CHALLENGING

Getting out of our comfort zone a little bit puts us on the right path. Challenges provide clarity. But they also help inspire us to keep going and to get through the difficult times. Small achievements. Big achievements. They're all important. They keep us moving forward, one step at a time.

The point of getting a little uncomfortable with a challenge is to give yourself signposts—a picture of Drago in a mirror—to keep yourself going. Keep your momentum toward success by challenging yourself in an achievable and realistic way.

But "a goal properly set is halfway reached," as Zig Ziglar once said. Because you'll be challenging yourself, you'll never be able to achieve *every single* thing you set out to achieve. It's just not realistic. (If you are achieving every goal you set, you need to challenge yourself more.) Somewhere along the way, failure is inevitable. They can be small or big. For some, there are "major failures" that seem too scary to overcome. It can stop our motivation and purpose dead in their tracks. But all are actually opportunities.

What's ironic is that failure feels like this big, negative thing. But it's vital for learning from our mistakes. In fact, you should expect failure as you attempt to achieve.

CHAPTER 8

FAIL IN ORDER TO SUCCEED

"Failure is simply the opportunity to begin again, this time more intelligently."

—HENRY FORD

Progress toward success is a constant cycle of learning, doing, *failing*, repeating, and then succeeding.

In the late nineteenth century, investors all around the world were racing to develop efficient electric lighting. Thomas Edison, known for his innovative and tireless work ethic as well as the many inventions attributed to him, dedicated himself to solving the problem.

To achieve his goal, Edison and his team at Menlo Park experimented with thousands of materials that could work as the filament—the key component of the light bulb. They tested everything from bamboo, cotton, hickory, and carbonized cardboard to vulcanized fiber, cork, fishing line, flax, and many others. The goal was to find the material that was the perfect combination of bright, long-lasting, and cost-effective.

Experiments ran around the clock, each using different combinations of materials to find the right filament.

Around two years and 1,200 failed experiments later, Edison landed on carbonized bamboo. It could last thousands of hours, burned brightly, and was reasonably priced. For the next decade, Edison sold the world's first modern light bulb using that filament.

Twelve hundred failed experiments is a lot. So, of course, he was asked about the process that led to his invention of the light bulb. It was a loaded question, framed to him as if he had wasted a lot of time and energy, like he was a failure. Edison famously said, "I did not fail. I found ten thousand ways that won't work." This sentiment encapsulated his philosophy that failure is not an end point but a crucial part of innovation and progress. Or, as philosopher Samuel Beckett wrote, "Ever tried. Ever failed. No matter. Try again. Fail again. Fail better."

Everything we do—even the things that we or others might deem a failure—gives us knowledge and experience that helps us carve a unique path to success.

COACHING FAILURE

My dad was a dedicated father, to put it mildly. He had eight kids, and he was involved in everything. I'll relegate it to sports, otherwise stories of his dedication would be book length. He coached every sport that I played, and the same was true for all my siblings.

When we were playing sports at school—where he wasn't the coach—that didn't deter him from being engaged with his kids. When I close my eyes, I can still see him sitting on the hood of his car watching practices or in the stands during games. Even though he was not on the sidelines, he very much wanted to let us know that he was there participating as our extended support system.

It was inspirational to me, so I've tried to emulate that when it came time for me to coach my own kids. And I have to say, I have no idea how my dad did it. It takes so much time and energy to coach.

When I first started coaching, it was for my oldest son's flag football team. In Texas, that starts around five years old. (Although, here in Texas, they'd start flag football the moment babies start to walk, if they could.) These kids were ragtag and didn't know the rules of the game. First down. Second down. Out of bounds. These were just words without meaning. If they had the ball, they would turn to run in the wrong direction or just throw it randomly or drop-kick it somewhere or roll around on the ground because, you know, getting dirty is fun.

I quickly realized that winning wouldn't be our primary goal. But I was the coach, so I needed to have some sort of program and set goals. I narrowed it down to two things: Have fun and get better. These were just small children, and I believed that these two goals were natural parts of their development.

We quickly embraced our collective failure. It would be okay for us to just constantly mess things up because that would happen regardless—that was just where they were at. But I decided that they needed to understand that whenever they messed up, whenever they failed, whenever they did something wrong, like chasing a butterfly instead of making the tackle, it was an opportunity for them to learn something. It was a teaching moment.

Those two rules—have fun and get better—allowed me to

simplify the coaching process and help them slowly build their skills. Now I apply the same principles to being a parent.

Let's face it, no one's perfect. I'm not the perfect parent. My kids are not the perfect kids. We are going to fail in those roles from time to time. But it's how we view and react to those failures that matters the most. Will they just occur and nothing changes, or will we use them to learn and get better?

The biggest mental hurdle that most people need to overcome is rethinking failure. It's not a "bad" thing, like most of us think. It feels like we've been implicitly taught our whole lives to avoid failure at all costs. That if you fail, you will be an outcast of society and laughed at mercilessly if you try to drive back into town to say hello. Failure is scary, or so we're taught.

But the truth is almost the opposite. Without the false starts, Edison wouldn't have learned what was required to invent the light bulb. Without failure, you won't find success. So, we should instead embrace failure as just another part of the learning and growth process. Sometimes touching a hot stove is the best way to learn not to do it.

Whether facing challenges within the grind or flat-out failing, these are opportunities and not roadblocks. Learn. Do. Fail. Repeat.

OF FEET AND FAILURE

That growth process tied to failure has followed me every step of the way in my podiatry career. Let's not forget that I wasn't even supposed to be a podiatrist. My original goal was to be a dentist like my father. When I failed to get into dental school, I had to embrace that experience and have the flexibility to adjust to podiatry.

After school, I faced more failure on Match Day, which

you may recall was when graduating medical students were picked by residency programs. My top choice was the program in Ohio, but they didn't even rank me. Failing to get into that program caused me to go to Texas and propelled me to succeed there.

But before the success of my practice, I was in the Houston-based residency program. That's when I learned what I thought success meant, at least from the point of view of most podiatrists. It apparently meant being a cutthroat—something I definitely wasn't. It meant joining the lecture circuit, teaching or directing education programs, innovating surgical techniques, or inventing new medical devices. For a while, it felt like these were the only options to find career success in podiatry. It wasn't until I entered into the real world of private practice that I was forced to learn how clipping toenails could actually pay off.

But even after I opened up my own practice, the failures kept coming. I made some mistakes on the business side of things. I used the wrong vendors, took bad advice, and hired the wrong people. Good help is very hard to find. I've chosen treatment regimens that may benefit the patient but can be cost prohibitive and decrease revenue for the business. Other approaches might not be best for the patient but tempt doctors to chase the dollar. I had to go through all of those mistakes and failures to build a better practice and stave off those larger mistakes that can implode a business.

Early on, I had a patient who had a very specific nerve surgery. It went very well. A year later, they wanted that same surgery done on the other side. When they came out of this second surgery, they were having weakness in their leg. There was nothing I could identify in the surgery that would have led me to believe there was something wrong. But, after the surgery, the patient had obvious and apparent problems that weren't there before. Even though I knew I didn't do anything wrong, I was still scared to death. And if I did do something wrong, I mentally prepared myself to make it right. It was shaping up to be a failure. Possibly small. Possibly practice-ending. Either way, I knew I was going to learn from it and correct it going forward.

I went in to see them, and we had a long discussion about how the surgery went and the symptoms surrounding their new symptoms. We quickly figured out that the tourniquet that was placed on their thigh likely weakened a nerve. I assured the patient of the temporary nature of the problem and spent extra time to let them know that I would do what I must to make sure things went right. In the end, the patient recovered successfully. It was a minor heart attack moment, but I learned that even potentially big problems can be fixed with good communication, genuine care, and honesty. I also learned the probability of going my entire career without a mistake was impossible. It was a good reminder about the importance of failure.

And, it should be mentioned, we are *all* failures. Even the greatest among us. And we all have the capacity to use those failures as opposition or as opportunities.

THE GREATEST PRESIDENT WAS ALSO A GREAT FAILURE

It is a matter of record that before becoming one of America's greatest presidents, Abraham Lincoln faced and overcame many failures. Let us count the ways.

Before becoming president of the United States was even a whisper in Lincoln's mind, he first attempted to succeed in business. Borrowing money, he bought a general store in New

Salem, Illinois, in 1832. His new venture wouldn't last long. It only took a year for Lincoln to fail as a businessman, having to shutter his store in 1833. To add insult to injury, he owed $1,000 to his creditors (roughly $38,000 in 2025). It took him seventeen years to complete payments.

The next time you lose your job, which is something I do not wish upon you, at least keep in mind that it was a circumstance that was one step in Lincoln's journey to becoming one of history's most important people.

Okay, so Lincoln was a business failure. But his political success is pretty well known. What that legacy obscures is a long series of political failures that preceded his presidency. In nearly every office he ran for, he was first defeated before he was elected—and this never occurred at low levels of government. In 1832, he lost his bid to be elected to the Illinois General Assembly. Staying resilient, he ran again in 1834 and won. When it was time to try his hand at the US House of Representatives, he lost twice before finally getting elected. And although he made the attempt to jump from the House to the US Senate, he ran two unsuccessful Senate campaigns. He never became a senator.

But Lincoln wasn't done failing. Next, he threw his hat into the ring for vice president. At the Republican National Convention in 1856, he was nominated with several others to be considered the vice presidential nominee on the Republican ticket. He was finished, kaput. Kidding, obviously. Four years later, he was elected president.

Despite all of these challenges, he never gave up. The challenging parts of his life taught him leadership, resilience, and the importance of perseverance. His story is proof that failure isn't an end point; it's a necessary step toward success.

Oh by the way, guess what your success rate is in the face of failure? If you're reading this, it's 100 percent. You're still here. You're still moving. And that's despite the challenges you've faced. So keep picking yourself up, keep learning, and keep resiliently moving forward on your path to success.

BOUNCING BACK WHEN YOU HIT THE BOTTOM

"The only real mistake is the one from which we learned nothing," Henry Ford once famously said. Those who succeed will learn from a catastrophic failure and pick themselves back up.

In fact, Ford's first company went bankrupt. It was called the Detroit Automobile Company, and it lasted for three years before it went under. What happened? Historians noted that the company was too focused on creating the perfect automobile. It was costing him too much money, taking too long, and didn't align with consumer needs. The company collapsed, and he hit rock bottom. But that didn't cause Ford to allow his name to be left out of the history books. It's like George S. Patton said, "Success is how high you bounce when you hit bottom."

He went back to the drawing board, recognized his mistakes, learned from them, and founded the Ford Motor Company. The new business model was to make something more affordable and streamlined. That way, the product would be available to middle-class Americans, a much larger customer base.

Before long, he was inspired to invent the assembly line as part of this streamlined process. Able to make cars at the scale of mass production, he more or less single-handedly created the industrial revolution.

Ford's failure with the Detroit Automobile Company pushed him naturally in the direction he needed to go. His company didn't succeed because of expense and lack of efficiency, so his next company focused on less expensive and more efficient. Without that setback, we'd still be riding around in horse-drawn carriages and buggies. Ford's story underscores the importance of resilience and using failure as a stepping stone to greater achievements.

THE J-CURVE

Most companies, big or small, undergo a process that isn't quite failure *just prior* to success. It's called the J-curve. It's a principle that states things *must* go backward initially. That's especially true of startups.

When I started Allevio—a company that takes the business burden off the doctor and lets them focus on patient care—my partners all warned me about the J-curve. The idea is that it's impossible to start and be optimized right out of the gate. In order to improve a business, you first have to open your doors to get experience in the market. Sure, you can put your best foot forward, a foot I'll examine and see if it needs to have its toenails clipped. But, like most any treatment for any pathology, things often get worse before they get better.

When Allevio took a harder look at my own practice, they noticed a liability that needed to be addressed: My clinic owned all of the doctors' cars. I got in the habit of buying my house-call doctors Tesla Model 3s. These Teslas were fairly affordable. And since they were electric vehicles, my doctors would save on gas. It felt like a really cool perk to offer my doctors, a way to say thank you and welcome them to the team. It was also one of the ways I tried to differentiate myself from other practices in town.

I was on my way to the first meeting with Allevio's CEO, and I got a call from one of my doctors saying he couldn't make the meeting because he'd just gotten into a wreck with his company Model 3. Not shortly thereafter, the CEO pulled me aside to talk about the cars, ownership, insurance, and liability.

This was the perfect example of me having good intentions that, when you did the math, caused a much bigger problem. It was just a huge liability. But the well-intentioned mistake of buying these cars meant that the company would be liable if anything were to happen. To correct that mistake, things had to get worse before they could get better. First, I had to take all the cars back. Obviously, that was not a popular move.

But I decided to take the cars back in a way that the doctors would be okay with, or, at least, in a way where they felt like they weren't getting the candy taken right out of their hands. In J-curve terms, that was a pretty contentious moment of pain for a lot of people. To propel the company culture forward again, we ended up giving the doctors car stipends. They could go out and buy whatever kind of car they wanted instead of being limited to one model, and then they would retain ownership and insurance themselves. The doctors were all very pleased with that outcome, and we can still use the stipend to differentiate ourselves from others. From a mistake, I learned then reiterated. What felt like a setback ended up being something that improved the clinic.

Part of the J-curve means living through the growing pains to get better. Everything that happened with these doctors' cars—from the initial excitement of them receiving cars, to making it the norm of my clinic, to identifying a liability issue, to taking back the cars, and then concluding with adding a car stipend—*all* had to happen in order for the business to improve. To fix issues and grow beyond, we first have to identify the problems, take a few steps back, then propel ourselves forward more effectively the next time around.

THE MATH OF FAILURE

In addition to the geometry of the J-curve, failure really does have a math to it. My work in Mexico really helped me understand the importance of resilience in the face of failure.

I was part of a group that would just go out and look for people who were in need of service and help them. It could be anything. Maybe they wanted help cleaning out their refrigerator. Maybe their house needed to be repainted in the aftermath of fire damage. Anything.

We would go door-to-door and just, very simply, let them know that we had arrived to help them with anything they needed. Sounds like a really easy concept. But it turned out that it was extremely difficult to help anybody.

Nine times out of ten, nobody would answer the door or whoever answered the door brought, let's say, not the kindest attitude to the conversation. Not infrequently, we'd get chased off. We would knock on a lot of doors and walk a lot of miles.

As time went by, we were met with abundant rejections. Naturally, I wanted to figure out a way to be more successful. Since our approach was very similar to door-to-door salesman—with the cold doorbell ring being the point of contact—I started researching successful door-to-door sales methods. Along the way, I ran into some surprising statistics. Only 10 percent of people tend to answer their door in the first place. And of that group, you can expect to "close" with 2 percent. That means somebody would be turned down five hundred times before getting a "yes."

Finding this out completely changed my mindset. Being told "no" didn't really sting as much as it did before, now that I knew that I should expect five hundred noes before getting a yes. I turned that repetitive rejection—that routine failure—into a game of math. I'd start going over it in my head: *"This* many people have already turned me down today, so I'm getting *this much* closer to somebody accepting my help."

After that, every time we were turned down, we would politely thank them for answering and listening and quickly move on. We needed hundreds more noes. I soon found out that my attitude and presentation changed toward what I previously perceived as a negative interaction. Because I started expecting to hear "no," I felt much more confident and comfortable with the doorstep pitch. I found that I started getting more and more yeses and that average of five hundred expected rejections started getting smaller. The math of failure became motivational, in a way. It was the catalyst that kept me going, a step ahead.

Pushing past setbacks can become a habit that creates resilience and persistence. In that way, and as stated by actress Aisha Tyler, "Success is not the absence of failure, it's the persistence through failure."

I started looking forward to the unanswered doors because they were better than having it slammed in my face. And those unanswered doors piled up quickly, getting me closer and closer to that one door that would accept my service.

Success, it turns out, requires a specific amount of failure. So don't let it demoralize you or prevent you from taking action. Do just the opposite. Leverage the math of failure to reveal the path to success.

LEARNING FROM THE "FAILURE" OF OTHERS—PART 1

Our own mistakes aren't the only beneficial forms of failure. We can also grow by witnessing how others respond to it. It's helped me navigate my career and find ways to thrive.

As I've mentioned, there is a honeymoon phase in podiatry where new doctors tend to stay at the first gig for only three to five years. For a variety of reasons, associates become dissatisfied with their original working conditions and start looking for a new role elsewhere. By and large, I consider this a failure of career preparation, one I tried to avoid myself by starting a practice.

Because of this occupational phenomenon, I expected my associates to experience the same thing. A revolving door of associates at my practice wouldn't instill trust, continuity, and community service. This systemic failure could damage its reputation and slow the progress and growth of my practice. So, how could I thwart this honeymoon issue within my own organization?

By the time the original contract was up for my associates, I had new agreements ready to go that were based on long-term stability, incentive programs, and other factors that were meant to address the most common needs of physicians. I even encouraged them to participate in the renegotiation process with an emphasis on making sure their work continued to align with their goals. I wanted to cultivate a work environment where my associates had agency. By learning from a systemic failure within podiatry, I was able to make an adjustment without first having to experience the damage myself. I've never lost a first-time associate doctor in my career. In fact, my doctors are known for their loyalty and consistency among all of Allevio's clinics. It has been critical to the success of my practice but also to the careers of my doctors.

Even if there are no easily discernable and common failures or mistakes within your own field or profession, that doesn't mean you can't look to others to learn. I find that tapping into pop culture or learning from people in careers outside my own can be extremely useful when learning from others' mistakes.

One of my favorite instances of taking influence from somebody in another career is the story of Mike Rowe. You may know him; he's the long-time host of *Dirty Jobs*, the television show that educates the viewer on lesser-known, extremely important, and potentially unpleasant-to-the-average-person occupations. The show is a celebration of these jobs but also of the work ethic of those who take these jobs. Maybe clipping toenails will appear in a future version of the show.

Before he became nationally famous, Mike Rowe's first gig was with *Evening Magazine* for a San Francisco affiliate. He was the on-site guy. The person they would throw it over to out in the field.

While employed there, he pitched an idea to the producers. Both his father and grandfather were tradesmen, and he thought it would be valuable to the community of viewers to celebrate blue-collar folks. So he asked a producer if he could do a story on a local sewer company and the ins and outs of what a day looks like for their laborers. The producer gave the green light, and the segment was shot. After submitting the segment, sewers were apparently too gross for the show. Shortly thereafter, he was fired and saw his career as an on-site anchor as a failure.

But, as is now well known, his concept was picked up by the Discovery Channel, which led to a decade-long run as one of the most popular shows on television. When I see that his success and achievements are predicated on a major setback, that's inspirational to me. It helps me push past the challenges that seem daunting to me. I learn that failure is not something unique to me. It unites us all.

LEARNING FROM THE "FAILURE" OF OTHERS—PART 2

When we learn from the failure of others, we avoid learning the hard way. And sometimes, learning the hard way can be a major setback.

When we think about the "learn, do, fail, and repeat" cycle, learning from others essentially eliminates the "fail" from that process. So it's extremely valuable to observe the mistakes and failures of others in order to internalize lessons that they've already revealed for us.

For example, I came across a podiatry group that was extremely successful and provided excellent care to their patients. They had a great business model, but one minor regulatory issue almost put them out of business.

Okay, I thought. *It's imperative to make sure I have every single license I need and am compliant with all regulations.* After witnessing that happen, I learned a crucial lesson without having to suffer the consequences myself. Thankfully, the owner is still going, trying to repair the negative impact that was created by this mistake. He didn't completely fold. He learned from it and is using that experience as part of his journey.

On a day-to-day level, it wasn't until I saw all of the mistakes and failures of others within podiatry as a resident that I made the conscious decision to clip toenails for a living. As you now know, podiatrists can fall into the career misconception that it seems more glamorous to focus on surgery. But with surgery, you're obviously doing a much more invasive treatment for the patient with a higher risk of a negative outcome. For me, it's difficult to think that what's best for the patient is cutting them open. It is my viewpoint that surgery should always be the last option. It's important, but it should be the last option. Anything that can get better without surgery should get better without surgery. I like to proudly say that my doctors get people better without having to do surgery. But I want to make clear that this is just my own medical style.

And reimbursements for surgeries in podiatry are smaller than most people would expect. A bunion surgery, perhaps the simplest podiatry surgery, earns a few hundred dollars, for example. And these surgeries are much more labor intensive, taking longer than other forms of treatment.

Then the doctor's liability goes way up for several reasons. First, you're doing higher-risk procedures. Then you're married to the patient for the ninety-day global period.

Knowing what my goals were financially for my practice, all of these norms in podiatry would have set me up for failure. They just didn't align with what I wanted to do. I can look at the discomfort other clinics experience with liability from surgery and learn from that without myself having to feel that discomfort.

My preference, in response, was to focus on preventative care—the proverbial clipping toenails. But that was, and probably still is, considered beneath podiatrists. It's looked down on to some degree, and many refuse to do it. It'll be outsourced to a nurse or physician assistant.

What many podiatrists consider success and failure was not consistent with what I thought. By perceiving it a failure not to pursue a business on the bread and butter of podiatry, I was able to adapt and grow my practice faster.

The good news is that anyone can implement the same strategy—of learning from others. When my older sibling got in a minor fender bender as a teenager and lost his driving privileges, eight-year-old me took that lesson forward, knowing to be extremely careful while driving so as to not have my dad take away the car keys. No doubt you've done something similar, and now it's time to put that experience into practice for your professional life.

VALUE YOUR FAILURES

This is where I'd like to return to my snowmobile accident. Many people around me perceived this as a major setback on my part. What I came to recognize is that experience was extremely critical for my learning. It taught me to be patient, to use two steps back to take three steps forward, to be resilient, to work hard in the face of anything, and that you can learn from *anything*, good or bad.

Accelerating your unique journey to success could be as simple as a change in perspective. Rather than a big, scary thing to avoid, think of failure as part of the process. When you fail, ask yourself this question: *What am I supposed to learn from this process?* That simple mindset shift allowed my snowmobile accident to give me gifts that would serve me in the future to propel my professional success.

On the other hand, setbacks can be complex and big. That doesn't change the fact that they are opportunities. Just look at SpaceX. Elon Musk's company spends quite a bit of money testing. But it's not a waste. When the debris has landed, the scientists sift through it with curiosity. They frame their approach with questions like, "What did we learn? How can we do this better next time?" It creates a cycle of learning, iterating, identifying mistakes, learning, and reiterating. Big or small, failures are failures. We can learn from them and fix them for the next time.

When approached the right way, failure can create patience, perspective, grit, and resilience. Failures can provide the lessons that help us overcome the next challenge successfully.

With that in mind, success itself is relative. What success means to one person will be completely different from another, and they'll both be valid and correct in their thinking.

PART 3

THE PROCESS OF SUCCESS

CHAPTER 9

DEFINE YOUR OWN SUCCESS

"Success is a journey, not a destination. The doing is often more important than the outcome."

—ARTHUR ASHE

There is no singular definition of success.

What's more, success is a process, not a product. It's not a landing pad where, once you've arrived, your journey is over. It's the discipline of showing up, failing, refining, and growing. Success can be *making* your own cookie dough, not just whether or not the cookies taste good.

If you didn't know how to make cookies a day ago but did it, you've just become successful. They don't have to be Martha Stewart level right away. Maybe you were trying to make a "healthy" batch with black beans but quickly learned the results weren't that great. It doesn't matter. The process of iterating, learning, and reiterating will help you define your own success.

You may recall the lessons I imparted on my son's football

team: If you are enjoying what you do and endeavor to progressively get better, you are successful! In fact, enjoyment and progress may be the universal principles to success. How can one argue that if you're enjoying something and getting better, that's not successful? From that framework, you get to make your own recipe.

Making cookie dough is as much an opportunity to be successful as running a company. Your recipe might not yield tasty results at first, but just keep iterating. If your goal is to write a book, like mine is with these words, that first book might end up being a hot mess. It might sell a million copies. It doesn't really matter. In the end, *you wrote a book*. It was printed. It was bound. It had a cover. With the next book, it's an opportunity to improve. The third book is another chance to get even better. Success is a process of learning, enjoying, and iterating again in an endless cycle.

In many ways, that never-ending cycle of staying engaged, learning lessons along the way, and transforming describes what it's like being a parent. When I had my first child, it became clear to me that I didn't always know what I was doing. I was flying blind, and I was building the plane as I was flying it, as they say. And I didn't always know what I was doing.

Whenever I would acknowledge to my first child, Noble, that my success as a father was *in process*, he and I were better able to find common ground on things. He didn't expect perfection from me, and I didn't expect perfection from him. That helped us quickly come together and apologize if we did something wrong.

The most important lesson I learned from the crash course that is parenting was this: It's okay to not know what you're doing. In other words, being a successful parent is more about trying to improve rather than being perfect.

The *Oxford English Dictionary* defines success as "the accomplishment of an aim or purpose." Who am I to argue with the *OED*, but I would at least like to create a dialogue. When I think about success, I don't think of it as the destination of an accomplishment. Instead, I'd like to zoom in on the *OED*'s inclusion of the words *aim* and *purpose*. To me, success is more about an ongoing process of always having an aim or a purpose, regardless of what's been accomplished.

Then, as you're mixing your own recipe with an aim or purpose big or small, the process to success itself could include other strategies that have worked for me, such as staying open, not being the smartest person in the room, taking on the dirty work of the grind, having a readiness to adjust on the fly, leveraging the J-curve, and putting yourself on the path to achieving goals.

What those goals are will be unique to you and what makes up your unique path to success. Maybe, for you, success is being a good parent, owning your own business, hitting a certain revenue threshold, being "the best" in your field, having a comfortable income, or literally anything else. You get to decide.

It doesn't matter what you do or what your goals are. Just do them well. Success is not an outcome. I've said it once, and I'll say it again: What we do matters less than *how* we do it.

SUCCESS IS NOT A MOMENT, BUT A PROCESS

Nobody achieves greatness or success overnight. It's just not a thing. Success is the result of a long process, usually yearslong or decades-long. It's not like Michelangelo was offered the gig to paint the Sistine Chapel—one of the most famous frescoes in the history of the world—on his first day as a painter. No. He had decades of study, persistence, hard work, and refinement under his belt.

But the bulk of his notable work up until that time was sculpture. In fact, when he was offered to paint the Sistine Chapel, he initially hesitated out of fear. He didn't consider himself a painter. You read that right. One of the most famous artists in human history had imposter syndrome and worked thinking that he was a failure. Who knew that many of us had imposter syndrome in common with Michelangelo. Thankfully, he implemented self-discipline and resilience in the face of those fears in order to give the world his art.

And it's not like he overcame the fear once and moved on. He worked for four years on the Sistine Chapel, painting tirelessly, learning and mastering new techniques, and used the opportunity to better himself. It was an enormous personal challenge.

And we are all very aware of the results—the successful results—of Michelangelo's Sistine Chapel. True success like his comes from a process of sustained effort over a longer period of time and not some sort of single defining moment.

While we have classic artists in mind, for me, another standout example of somebody who approached their work as a process was (my other favorite ninja turtle) Leonardo da Vinci. He's remembered as one of history's greatest polymaths—an artist, scientist, engineer, and thinker.

Da Vinci often left paintings unfinished or pursued projects that had no immediate practical application. His notebooks are filled with anatomical sketches, engineering designs, and scientific observations—many of which were centuries ahead of their time. His success was not about producing but about his lifelong process of exploration.

He didn't limit himself to being one specific thing or abide by any social expectations. He focused less on *what* he did and more on *how* he approached everything. That approach was with rigorous observation, detailed study, and innovative thinking. Whether designing a flying machine or painting the *Mona Lisa*, da Vinci's success was in his method rather than a specific field.

It's his approach to learning and problem-solving that have made him a transcendent figure of humanity. He demonstrates that success is not about a finished product but about continuously refining one's craft, questioning assumptions, and embracing the process of discovery. It's why he remains influential across multiple disciplines, centuries after his death.

What your process is and what techniques you need to learn on the job and master will depend on your unique journey. For me, it was clipping toenails for a living.

CLIP TOENAILS FOR A LIVING

One of my joys in life is to answer the question, "What do you do for a living?" Without pause I'll reply, "I clip toenails for a living," layering descriptive details about the fungal, brittle, ingrown, thickened, and discolored nails I look at daily. I might mention spending hours each week driving the Greater Houston area to enter someone's home, sit on their dirty floor, and maneuver my face close to these kinds of nails in order to evaluate and treat the human foot.

It's a decidedly, purposefully, and truthfully unglamorous answer. Most of the time, the listener's eyes widen in confusion. Their contorted visage makes me presume they're thinking, *Is he joking?* I enjoy the skepticism and confusion that's elicited from my response, as if I'm making it all up. Surely nobody would make a conscious decision to clip fungal toenails in a stranger's bathroom for a living.

However, this exchange is always a great opportunity to showcase my beliefs about success. Success doesn't have to mean graduating from Harvard, climbing the ladder at a Fortune 500 company, developing world-changing innovations, or being recognized by your peers. It could mean any of those things for you, but it doesn't have to.

There is no singular strategy, blueprint, or recipe for success. But what it *does* require is that you define success for yourself and then embrace the ongoing process that helps you inch ever closer to that goal. You can be lazy successfully if that is your aim or purpose. Or you can work to retire early. It doesn't matter. Successful oatmeal raisin cookies will taste much different than successful peanut butter cookies, but they are both successes.

Be wary if you come across anything that has *the* blueprint on how to achieve success because it's not a one-size-fits-all situation. It's not like a LEGO set, for example. When I build LEGOs with my children, the package includes a step-by-step guide on how to go from a big pile of blocks to the finished toy. No matter who is putting this LEGO set together, everybody will build it the same way and reach the same result. In my experience, that's not applicable to individual hopes and dreams. It's not how the world works.

What's worked for me is a combination of unique goals, grit, flexibility, and the other traits I've outlined in this book. For you, that process could be totally different. You get to define success for yourself.

For me, one definition of success means clipping toenails for a living. What is your definition? Find your toenails. Then clip them. And do it well.

WHATEVER YOU DO, DO IT WELL

In terms of doing something well, the story of Kalani Sitake's father is an inspirational one. For those of you who don't know, Kalani Sitake is the head football coach of BYU. (Go, Cougars!) Brigham Young University is also his alma mater, and he spent time in the NFL with the Cincinnati Bengals. Currently, Sitake has the second-highest head coach winning percentage in BYU's history. Suffice to say, the guy is successful.

And for Coach Sitake, success runs in the family. I was lucky enough to hear him tell the story of his father. His father worked as a custodian and would sometimes take his sons with him.

One specific night, Coach Sitake's dad brought him and his brother to work just after a large number of staff had been laid off. The sons helped their dad late into the night clean and organize the offices from the remnant chaos of the mass layoffs. What was now clean was once papers strewn about, objects kicked over, and other evidence of a clear bedlam in the rush out the door.

At the end of the shift, father and sons looked over the office to take pride in how organized and clean everything was. But he gave the boys one last task. He asked them to take his keys, lock up the office, and then deposit the keys in an overnight box because he wouldn't be needing them anymore. That was his last day at work, too. He had been laid off with dozens of others. As their father said this, his face swelled with pride.

Even on his last day at work, Coach Kalani's father instilled in him and his brother that one's job matters no matter the circumstances. Giving 100 percent effort, even when it's not expected, is a form of success.

Coach Kalani recalled this moment as being a foundational learning experience for him. It impacted him greatly, and he credits it with giving him the work ethic to achieve the various successes he's had in football. Whatever you do—be it collegiate coaching or custodial work—do it well. And be content with whatever success you find and *how* you find it, even if it's not on a traditional path.

An example of a traditional path might be getting a college education. It's a ubiquitous cultural narrative to the point that, for many kids, not going to college feels stigmatizing. For my own children, I never thought that they should feel forced to take that traditional educational path. If they want to pursue a trade, that's fine with me. My oldest son recently defined what success would look like in his own career path. He wants to become a commercial airline pilot.

He's really latched onto it and is already accumulating hours of flight. He won't need a college degree to achieve his goal. Instead, he'll need a private pilot license and a valid FAA medical certificate (a physical that deems he is fit enough to fly). He'll need to pass written and practical exams, obtain a multiengine rating through instruction and flight tests, and log a specific number of flight hours.

Despite not falling into the narrative of a traditional education, he has a clearly defined path to success complete with incremental goals to achieve along the way. He understands that it doesn't matter what you do or what it takes to get there, you just have to do it and do it well. And I'm proud of that.

He could change his mind and pursue something else. And that would be fantastic, too. I'd be proud of him for making that adjustment. It doesn't really matter what he chooses; I know he'll try to be the best at it and be content with whatever success he finds. Success, after all, is relative.

TO BE RICH, OR TO BE KING

Relative success means you get to define it for yourself. Even so, we have to be realistic about what's achievable. Do you want to be rich? Do you want to be king?

In healthcare today, it seems like all specialities and successful small practices are getting gobbled up by larger groups. Whether that's private equity or large hospital entities, that's the way things have been going.

My *C*—my planned reward—had always been to sell my practice. I was going to build something from nothing and then exit. Well, around the time that larger entities were starting a buying craze, I thought, *This is probably going to be the best way to sell*. That's when I decided to sell my practice to start a podiatry management company, Allevio.

Around the time I was selling my practice, an investor in Allevio shared Noam Wasserman's book, *The Founder's Dilemmas*. In it, Professor Wasserman argues that you can be rich or you can be king but not both. You can have control or you can have generational wealth but not both. So you have to make a choice based on your preferences.

It's a decision that, I think, every business owner has to make. My dad made the choice he wanted to make. He was king, and he didn't want to grow any bigger than his single practice. It's not right or wrong. That was his *C*. For me, I knew that I wanted to grow a practice like my father and then replicate it on a larger scale. I wanted to expand my practice nationally but knew I didn't have the means or skillset to grow it beyond where it had gotten. So I sacrificed control and took the action more aligned with my *C*.

You'll have to make a similar choice.

Growing up, I was lucky enough to watch my dad's work ethic as a dentist. I was lucky to work the family farm to cultivate my own work ethic. Through it all, I realized that in order to achieve, hard work was necessary. The rewards and the consequences you sew stem from your actions, effort, and vision. You can only get to *C* if you start plugging in the right *A*'s and *B*'s along the way. Power through, keep your feet moving one step at a time, and keep your momentum going.

But don't let the momentum become momentum for momentum's sake. (Say that three times fast.) We all have instances where we are just working, working, working and getting nowhere because of the blinders we've put on. So, how can we optimize our efforts to maximize our rewards? One answer might be in standing out from the crowd.

SUCCESS IS RELATIVE

We get to determine our own definition of success. And just because your success *could* be perceived to be lesser than something else's out there, don't let that deter you from staying on your own defined path.

I think of social media influencers who post to TikTok, Instagram, and everything else. These folks are showing the world only the best parts of their lives—or a carefully curated version of their struggles. These narratives don't show the reality of living as a process. They don't show the mundane daily routines, negative feedback, financial concerns, arguments, self-doubt, and other common components to the long-haul process of success.

You don't need to compare your goals to their lives. Sure, the appearance of success can breed more success. I've found that to be true. But it can also be true that comparing ourselves to others who are successful creates a negative feedback loop that shifts our focus away from ourselves. When that happens, it'll be easier for us to spiral out of the standards we've set for ourselves. Comparison can destroy motivation, so just be careful.

In fact, many things that appear rough around the edges are actually success stories. Earlier, I mentioned the story of when my wife and I went to sell our first house, and it applies again here. All of the prospective buyers gave us the same feedback: The house looked really lived in. We both laughed because the house was only three years old.

We had painted it and freshened it up like any seller would. But there was no hiding how hard my family had lived in that house. It may have cost us a little bit of money when going to sell, but to me that feedback was a huge success. I felt like, *We're doing something right*. What buyers viewed as a failure on our part was actually a success. We had filled that space with love, play, hard work, and interconnectivity.

It might not be as "successful" a home sale as it could have been. I don't choose to define that home's success by how much it sold for. That home was a success because of the memories we made there.

Selling this house taught me another important lesson: I was already successful, but I just didn't know it. By and large, people are actually very successful and they may not recognize that about themselves.

Consider this. Where you are right now is part of the success journey and process that is unique to you. You may feel like you are at a point of failure, but the reality might be different. You have success lying around. Leverage those things to propel yourself forward.

You could be in the J-curve. Maybe you've been rejected from dental school or have to sell your house for less money than you thought. But that's a pulled-back bow ready to launch you forward.

When you define your own success, it gives you the target to shoot for. To stay in flight, make success a process of learning, doing, failing, succeeding, and then starting the process all over again. Now it's your turn to take aim.

CHAPTER 10

ALWAYS TAKING ACTION

"The way to get started is to quit talking and begin doing."
—WALT DISNEY

What ensures success isn't passive knowledge but an active pursuit. Success is a cycle of action—some mix of challenging yourself, seeing the value of the fundamentals, getting motivated in discomfort, working hard, standing out from others, surrounding yourself with amazing people, knowing when and how to pivot, using your mistakes as an opportunity to learn, and then doing that over and over again.

You may find some or one of these ingredients helpful when crafting your own recipe of success. Consider it a choose your own adventure. For me, each has been vital. To achieve that success, I've used the core principles I've outlined in this book. But there's one more that I want to explore, and that's being open to opportunities.

What does that mean, really? A lot of people will sometimes

try to lessen or write off their success as "being at the right place at the right time." It's a good turn of phrase, but it carries with it some notion that success just happens to us randomly or accidentally. Many would call it being lucky or blessed.

The truth is that being in the right place at the right time takes work—all of the elements of success we've covered—*and* the ability to, at any moment, take action immediately. When opportunities fall into our lap, it's because those around us know that we are the right person for that opportunity. Make the most of those opportunities.

OPPORTUNITIES FALL INTO YOUR LAP

At the time of writing, I marked the ten-year anniversary of my snowmobile accident. And on the very same calendar weekend I was injured, I found myself flying back to Utah. It was a little scary. But it gave me pause to reflect on the journey that it sent me on—the adjustments and grind that it took to regain movement to my current work with Allevio.

When I brought on my first associate, it was the first step in growing my practice. Little did I know that it would also help me weather the storm of recovery from my snowmobile accident.

I wanted to be the best at house calls and clipping toenails. I wanted to do my best within my career—differentiating myself with the bread and butter of podiatry to eventually grow the business to sell. I used house calls and toenails to build my first associate's patient base. I was able to leverage the abundance of patients from house calls into more and more growth.

A few years after my first associate, I brought on two more associates. I opened a clinic with one and bought an existing clinic for the other. It didn't happen overnight, but it did start with my palms facing upward to catch the opportunities. Thomas Jefferson once said, "I find that the harder I work, the more luck I seem to have." And that is certainly true of the opportunities that have found me and will find you.

I met the second associate at the end of December while I was in surgery. A colleague came into the operating room and said, "You're not going to believe this, but I've got a doctor here visiting me from Huntsville who wants to open a practice there. I know that you're thinking about opening up a clinic there because it's near your new ranch house. I'll get you two connected." After the surgery, I went in to meet him to get more information. He wanted to open a clinic in his hometown but didn't want to have to run a business. He was a hard worker and had deep ties to the local community. That's just the person you want to surround yourself with. And he was graduating at a time that aligned with when I wanted to open this satellite clinic.

Collaborating to set some goals, this young doctor and I decided we would replicate the model I had used in my very first clinic. After that, we quickly found a place that we could sublease in Huntsville; it was inexpensive but provided a brick-and-mortar facility to see patients. The total cost to open this new clinic required less than $12,000 of capital, and it operated on around $2,500 a month, nearly a quarter of my main clinic.

Just like my own clinic, we created a system where he would build his patient base by doing house calls three days a week and being in the clinic two days a week. We started with zero patients but always had a need for house calls. That's how we got his clinic slowly growing. Flash-forward to today, and his clinic is bustling at full capacity as my busiest clinic.

By the time I was able to open the next clinic, it was 2019, right around the time of the COVID-19 pandemic. Normally, podiatry residents would be doing externships or hospital rotations. But because of the situation, they were out looking for things to do. One resident who had their externship canceled reached out to me to ask if she could just shadow my practice for a week.

I said yes, again prepared with my palms up to catch the opportunity that fell my way. After spending some time in our clinic, everybody had a high regard for her immediately. In addition to being a great doctor, she was the nicest, friendliest, happiest, and most helpful person. Knowing the importance of surrounding my practice with good people, I told her that, when she started looking for a job, I hoped that she would consider our clinic as a possibility.

Meanwhile, this story also involves a *different* doctor who would do surgeries with me while she was in a local residency. She and I would talk about the business side of podiatry. She wanted to have her own practice after she graduated, and I was happy to help guide her in some of the business aspects of that process. She ended up buying a retiring doctors' forty-year-old clinic in Houston. A few years after she graduated, she reached out to me, telling me she was just about to take a job in another state and was looking to sell her practice. She wanted to sell it for basically the debt that was in it, and since I had helped mentor her before she bought it, she wanted to offer it to me. Having replicated my first clinic twice and needing to hire more doctors for house calls, I agreed, my palms up and ready.

At this point, I knew I was taking on multiple growth projects at once, but I understood that most things that are worth doing require hard work. I bought that doctor's low-risk, steady practice for its debt. It turned out that the practice I bought had a very highly sought-after contract with one of the closed-panel insurance companies in Texas. The rule was that they only had one provider per speciality per zip code. But since I now owned this practice, all of my other practices could differentiate themselves by utilizing this contract, enabling astonishing growth.

From there, I thought this would be the perfect incentive to hire the outstanding doctor who had just finished shadowing me. She agreed to be my new associate, helping take on some of the abundant house call referrals, and she was excited to have the opportunity to make a new clinic her own.

So there I was, in quick succession, going from one clinic to three, from two doctors to five! I also added three part-time doctors who worked for other practices around Houston to help take on some of these house calls. These opportunities were possible because I had harnessed the easy and underserved work within my scope and implemented other core ingredients of success. There were difficulties to overcome, but there were also known benefits from the willingness to take on the opportunity.

These successes came from the discomfort and in experiencing the ups and downs—the failures and mistakes—of both buying an existing clinic and opening a new satellite clinic. It was a J-curve that launched me rapidly forward.

PLAYING THE CARDS YOU'RE DEALT

When you dream of opening a business, things always seem grander in your head than what happens in reality. That happened to me when I opened my first practice. I was going to be splitting my time between house calls and clinic work. But even though I wouldn't be in the office all but half of the week, I still wanted it to be a nice space.

I found a plastic surgeon who had a big, beautiful clinic

(complete with medispa) that he wasn't using for three days a week. He was out on surgery and was looking for somebody to sublease his space. I knew I was going to need a space three days a week but would use the other two doing house calls. It was a card that was dealt right to me. It felt like I should pick it up and play it.

I couldn't afford to rent his entire space for the three days a week, so he granted me use of two treatment rooms and allowed me to have a small "storage closet" that would double as my office. It wasn't the grandiose clinic space I had imagined—a bit of a setback—but it was something. And I could sublease for very little. Combining the pivot with embracing unglamorous work, I utilized that space three days a week while he was out for surgery.

Since then, and as you've been reading, I continued putting in the work, which led to expansion. I consider myself very fortunate, but you can only play the cards you are dealt if you get yourself to the table. This is all part of a "playing the cards you're dealt" strategy, which also includes anticipating what might happen in the future. Instead of just playing your opponent like in poker, you can also play your environment.

Near the time when my sublease with the plastic surgeon ended, I was asked to take over the lease of a vein doctor who passed away. His wife asked me if I'd be willing to take over the lease on my own. I moved upstairs to my own space on the second floor of that same building. That was extremely helpful for differentiation, branding, marketing, and all the things we couldn't do when we were in a space that wasn't really ours. Learning from the plastic surgeon, I strategically subleased part of my space to the nurse who worked for the deceased vein doctor. This helped me cover the cost of this new big space while I continued to grow.

For five years in this new space, I had my eye on a medispa that was right at the entrance of the building on the first floor. It had big, glass doors and a really nice-looking lobby. It was the type of space that would set anybody apart from other businesses, and I could tell that the landlords wanted to give an excellent first impression for the building with this space.

The owner of the medispa was a patient of mine. As time went on, she indicated their intention to move out and get a smaller space. After five years of anticipating this card being dealt, I patiently waited until it appeared. And I played it. I told her, "Before you do anything, let me talk to the building manager because I am really interested in taking over that space." By that time, I needed the extra space. It was during COVID-19, and guidelines lessened the amount of patients who could be in the clinic, thus more clinic space meant more patients. There was also a short period of time we would need to close down to work on and move into the new space. The timing of COVID-19 shutting everything in the world down provided me an opportunity to make this transition and upgrade my space. And, it should be noted, the demand for house calls had also exploded. In short, I needed to adapt in the face of the practice's growth.

So that's when we moved in as part of our new growth goals. And the building had a tenant allowance, helping us repaint and add floors that really made it our own. By doing that, we had more than doubled our size. This encouraged more growth, and we added four more providers into the clinics. That expanded us to twelve doctors, and we continued to be so busy that we had to acquire another suite in the same building that we used exclusively for running the house calls.

That led to the differentiation of the house call side of our business, which became Door Docs. We invested in branding the website and created a whole different compensation structure. The bread and butter of podiatry, an area in which I wanted to set myself apart from others, now had its own arm within my organization.

So, by being open to opportunities, working hard, adjusting on the fly, surrounding myself with smart people, having a vision of the future, and playing the cards I was dealt, my staff and I could become the best versions of ourselves that fostered continuous growth. Success became a process rather than some bottom line.

UPS AND DOWNS

But not everything on the path to success ends in some glorious result. There are mistakes, failures, and setbacks. Your path will look like a stock market performance tracker. Have you ever looked at the stock market on an hourly view? In one hour, a stock can peak, drop, spike, and nose-dive multiple times. Over sixty minutes, you might see a net loss in value. It dips and surges. If you zoom out to a daily, weekly, monthly, or even annual view, you can still see ups and downs, but you get a clearer picture of the stock value. But when you zoom out to a three- or five-year view, the S&P, Dow Jones, and NASDAQ all go up and in the positive direction over time. You can choose to zoom in on a daily or monthly dip and think it's a setback, but that will only do you more harm. It would lead to pulling your money out of the stock market before it rebounds. If you leave it in and keep working, you'll see your portfolio climb steadily.

Maybe there are times when you think you're not doing enough and not being the best version of yourself. If you zoom in too much, you're only seeing a myopic piece of your path to success. You must zoom out to understand that, along the journey to success, you will have ebbs and flows, gains and losses. That doesn't mean you are a failure. Think of your three-, five-, and ten-year journey. Or think about this. Your journey started in diapers. You were unable to walk or speak. Now look at you! It's all part of your unique path. The pullback on the arrow is necessary for the bow to launch it forward. Or, as actress Lily Tomlin puts it, "The road to success is always under construction."

YOU'RE NOT DONE

You'll always be in process. It's not like you ever reach an end point and are done achieving. There are no movie moments in life where you get a nicely wrapped-up ending to a feel-good story. Your story will continue until you can't breathe anymore.

In the face of growing a successful practice, my story continued, too. There are always new cards to play. In the fall of 2023, I was having lunch with someone who ended up being a co-founder of Allevio. I've known Casey for twenty years and really admire him. He's the type of person who inspires people to do their best by constantly trying to improve himself. He's a dedicated, walking-talking self-help book. The type of smart person you should surround yourself with.

He is a businessperson first and foremost, and he sold one of his startups to BlackRock, one of the world's largest private equity firms, for an amount that, let's say, would allow him to retire immediately. But he's never stopped, and he puts himself in a lot of environments looking for new opportunities, palms up and ready to work with what's in front of him, surrounding himself with the right people to allow his own continued growth.

I made house calls, and one of his first businesses was selling alarms door-to-door. So we had an affinity for each other since we shared (to some degree) a vocation. When he put two and two together—that I ran a successful business, he liked growing businesses, and that my business was similar to something he had already done—he called me on the phone.

I was in the middle of a pig hunt, and I had to stop my four-wheeler to see why my phone was vibrating. When I saw his name I thought, *Casey has never outright called me before.* That struck me enough to put off what I was doing and answer the phone. He wanted to know if I would be interested in him investing in my practice and that, if so, we could talk more later.

With my palms up ready to take another opportunity, he sent an analyst to follow me around for a month. All of my effort was about to turn into a reward because, when Casey called me back after the analyst left, he didn't just want to invest a little bit. He wanted to replicate my podiatry business model as a group. I was obviously open to the idea, happy that an ace of spades had been dealt into my hand to play.

Casey sent another consultant, Matt, now the CEO of Allevio, to conduct the due diligence. Matt immersed himself into the business, legal, billing, and regulation sides of my practice. Before Matt sent in his final report to Casey, he quietly indicated to me that he thought there was a lot of potential. He not only wanted to partner with me, but he wanted to help operate the entire playbook. That was the first time in my entire career where my reaction was, *Whoa.* It just goes to show that if you continue to put in the effort and take action, the process of success provides space for continued growth.

Within a few months of opening, Allevio was helping more than thirty podiatry clinics across the nation build and improve their practices. Our mission statement is to "empower healing anywhere." This large-scale healthcare endeavor was made possible by a humble, bread-and-butter practice of making house calls and clipping toenails.

At Allevio, our goal is to become the best podiatry group in the country, a challenging goal that helps us keep the process of success moving forward. Part of that process has led to continued training where we are working to build a curriculum that helps any doctors optimize their practice.

And that's where I'm at in my journey, currently. But it's not the end for me. The story will continue. Success is not a landing point; it's a journey. It's not the mountaintop. It's the climb. And the same is true for you. I've found a unique path and recipe that I'm still adding to. This is my version. Take what you want from my recipe and add it to yours until you find what's right for you. And keep adjusting as you go.

Although this book will have an actual end after you turn the last page, don't let yourself think that success functions the same way. It takes effort to get rewards. You have to consistently work toward it like a process because it *is* a process. It's so important, I'll reiterate it: Success is a journey and not the destination.

You might be on the upward or downward swing, but that's just a temporary phase. You might feel like you're fail*ing* or succeed*ing*, but the "ing" signifies that you are still in process. It's still ongoing.

To help encourage things to stay on the upward trajectory as much as possible, that means taking action consistent with principles of success to foster its growth. Choose your ingredients that make the most sense for your particular situation. If you're not certain, experiment a little and see what opportunities present themselves. If something isn't working, make an adjustment or embrace your field's bread and butter. Salt to taste.

Whether you know it or not, you *are* on the path. As your success process plays out, always focus on doing what you do well. It matters less if you are clipping toenails, driving a garbage truck, teaching a class of students, or running a private equity firm. Just do it well and find the resilience to move forward. If you're doing it well and differentiating yourself, you will have value.

Are you adapting to your circumstances? Are you working hard in spite of obstacles? Are you accepting failure and learning from it? Are you accepting opportunities with open palms? Are the people around you helping you improve? Have you identified your specific version of "clipping toenails for a living," or your specific version of success? These are the kinds of things to think about as you take your next action.

There will always be a next chapter for you, even after this one is done. And the next chapter of your life should focus on how to foster your unique success.

This isn't the end. This is a new beginning. Endeavor to continue writing *your* story.

ACKNOWLEDGMENTS

Above everyone else who I owe thanks, no one deserves more credit than my favorite person, Brittany. She put in more effort than anyone over the last twenty years to get our family where we are today. Her never-ending support through school, residency, and opening our practice matched her strength in overcoming so many of the challenges we faced. I love you.

Noble, Emmy, Holland, Bear, Robbie, and Rylynn, you all continually keep me learning and evolving. If I'm straight bussin' or yeetin' it, it's 'cause my kiddos are low-key GOATed and drippin' with sauce. Bet. 😎

To my mom and dad, I will never comprehend how you managed to raise the eight of us the way that you did. I am eternally grateful for your example, love, and selflessness. I strive to be a fraction of the parent that you both are.

My siblings. During my upbringing, you all easily had the biggest impact on me. When I talk about surrounding oneself with the best people, I mean you.

I have to praise my partner in writing this, Nicholas Potter. You have a great skill at untangling the knot of Christmas lights from my head to make sense of it. If not for you, this book would be in crayon, not ink. Thank you.

And I also want to thank Katie and Rachel, the rest of my Scribe team.

This idea was presented to me by my friend and partner, Casey Baugh. Thank you for your motivational jet fuel that thousands of people use to become better. No one is a better example of constant personal progress and greatness. You are one of one.

A special thanks to my podiatry partner Brian Conley. He picked up extra work so that I could execute this project. Thank you for being a sounding board and anchor in our practice.

A big focus of this book was to have someone in mind that you were aiming toward as your target audience. Riley, your "shop chats" helped me think of young professionals who could hear something in this book and find it beneficial. Your pranks also keep me on my toes.

Brent, thank you for the constant stream of advice and encouragement. Brenda, you're a saint.

Brian Christiansen, if I ever have self-doubt or feel inadequate, I think of you and how much you love and support me and my family. You have a special talent at making people feel good about themselves.

ABOUT THE AUTHOR

DR. MARCIN N. VACLAW is a foot and ankle specialist and the chief medical officer and founding partner of Allevio, LLC, a national podiatry managed service organization. He also acts as executive chairman of Allevio's Medical Advisory Board.

Allevio is one of the fastest-growing podiatry companies in the country and was born out of Dr. Vaclaw's Houston, Texas, clinics.

Dr. Vaclaw started his podiatry clinic from nothing more than ambition, a business plan, and implementing in-home visits. He grew it to become the largest group in Houston before founding Allevio with his business partners. He is humbled to be a partner with Matt Mathison, Casey Baugh, Dave Jenson, and Vivint's Todd Peterson.

Everything in his life revolves around his beautiful wife, Brittany, and their six amazing children. Together the Vaclaws love riding, training, and breeding horses at their private equestrian center in Texas. Dr. Vaclaw also enjoys running Heavenly Cattle Co., which breeds miniature Scottish Highland cows.

www.ingramcontent.com/pod-product-compliance
Lightning Source LLC
Chambersburg PA
CBHW030443090526
44586CB00044B/582